Principles of Business Road to Success Handbook
Updated CXC Syllabus
Ajillah Sinnette-Vincent

Copyright © 2020 Ajillah Sinnette-Vincent

All Rights Reserved. No part of this book may be reproduced, scanned, or transmitted in any forms, digital, audio, or printed, without the expressed written consent of the author.

Dedication

This book is dedicated to my parents, husband, daughters, and brothers. May my love for learning always be true.

Table of Contents

UNIT 1 — 10
NATURE OF BUSINESS — 10
- Bartering system — 10
- History of subsistence economy to money economy — 12
- Instruments of payments or exchange — 13
- Public and private sector — 18
- Types of business structures — 20
- Sole trader/sole proprietor — 21
- Partnership — 22
- Co-operatives(co-op) — 24
- Franchises — 25
- Private and public companies — 26
- Private limited company — 27
- Public limited company — 28
- Economic systems — 29
- Free Enterprise/Capitalist or Market Economy — 30
- Mixed economy or dual economy — 32
- Functional areas of a business — 33
- Stakeholders of a business — 34
- Legal & ethical issues in operating a business — 35
- Careers in business — 36

UNIT 2 — 38
INTERNAL ORGANIZATIONAL ENVIRONMENT — 38
- Management — 38
- Functions of management — 38
- Organizational chart — 40
- Leadership — 43
- Leadership styles — 43
- Internal source of conflict — 45
- Communication — 48

UNIT 3 — 49
ESTABLISHING A BUSINESS — 49
- An entrepreneur — 49
- Steps taken to establish a business — 51
- Reasons for starting a business — 52
- Difference between entrepreneur and entrepreneurship — 52
- Business plan — 53
- Market research — 54
- Feasibility study — 55
- Planning — 55
- Collateral — 56
- Ways the government can regulate businesses — 57

Factors affecting the location of a business ---57
UNIT 4 ---59
LEGAL ASPECTS OF A BUSINESS ---59
   Contract ---59
   Importance of record-keeping in a business ---63
   Business documents ---64
   Insurance ---68
UNIT 5 ---72
FACTORS OF PRODUCTION ---72
   Types of factors of production ---72
   Difference between production and productivity ---74
   Cottage Industries ---76
   Small business ---76
   Linkage industry ---77
   Effects of growth on a business ---78
   How a business grows internally & externally ---79
   Natural resources found in Caribbean countries ---79
UNIT 6 ---80
MARKETING ---80
   MARKET ---80
   Marketing ---80
   Factors influencing consumer behaviour ---83
   Factors affecting packaging and presentation of goods ---84
   Why consumer organizations exist ---86
   Terms of sale ---87
   The Role of Customer Service ---88
   Intellectual property rights ---90
UNIT 7 ---91
LOGISTICS AND SUPPLY CHAIN ---91
   Logistics ---91
   Supply chain operations ---91
   Activities in supply chain operations ---92
   Difference between multi-modal and intermodal transport ---93
   Modes of transport ---93
   Transport documents ---97
   Advantages and Challenges (disadvantages) of Supply Chain Operations --99
   Impact of information technology on logistic and supply chain operations ---100
   Forms of technology ---100
   How Logistic Contributes to the Competitiveness of Business ---101
   Party logistics ---102
   Global logistic providers ---102
UNIT 8 ---104
BUSINESS FINANCE ---104

- Financial institutions — 104
- Role of central banks over commercial banks — 106
- Services offered by financial institutions — 107
- Regulatory Bodies — 108
- What is the difference between savings and investments? — 110
- Short-term financing — 111
- Long-term financing — 112
- Financial records — 113

UNIT 9 — 115

RESPONSIBILITIES (ROLES) OF GOVERNMENT IN AN ECONOMY — 115
- Responsibilities of a government — 115
- Ways a government can influence businesses to protect the environment — 116
- Taxation — 117
- Forms of assistance offered by the government to businesses — 119

UNIT 10 — 121

TECHNOLOGY AND GLOBAL BUSINESS ENVIRONMENT — 121
- National income — 121
- How GDP, GNP, and NNP affect economic growth, economic development, standard to living and quality of life — 122
- International trade — 123
- Economic institutions in the region and globally — 124
- Major Economic Problems in the Caribbean and Solutions — 126
- Foreign investment — 127
- Business Technology — 128
- Consequences of unethical use of ICT — 131
- Factors that determine a country's standard of living and its quality of life — 132

UNIT 1
NATURE OF BUSINESS

Business is an organization with the utmost priority to generate some profit through the constant activity of providing goods and services to individuals and the public. The nature of business cuts across many professions that render different services, with their different professional business ethics. However, there are many systems used to run and operate a business, such as the bartering system.

Bartering system

This is a system of business that involves the direct exchange of goods and services without the use of money. It is as old as human civilization as it is regarded as the first type of trade. It is simply the exchange of goods for goods, and not for money. This system stems from the age of antiquity, and it has some merits and demerits.

Items exchanged in the barter system

1. Tangible items

These are the items that can be seen or touched. For example, craft items, food items, shells, beads, and peas.

2. **Intangible items**

These are the items that cannot be seen or touched. For example, singing, dancing, dressmaking, barbering, and baking.

Advantages of bartering

- ✓ Bartering allows one to possess items that he/she could not produce or possess initially.
- ✓ Surplus (excess) goods could be exchanged through the bartering system.
- ✓ It is very flexible and highly responsive as one can trade a related product for another without much ado. For example, trading a laptop for a portable tablet.
- ✓ It is an amazingly simple system to use because it requires little or no rules, scope, procedures, and criteria.

Disadvantages of bartering

1. **Lack of double coincidence of wants**

To barter, one finds a partner who is willing to barter with the item in need of. Most times, it is always difficult to get a partner who is willing to barter with the appropriate pressing item at a given time and situation. Oftentimes, this seems to be practically impossible.

2. **Lack of a common measure of value**

In the bartering system, there is no way of measuring the exact value of goods traded or services rendered. There is little or no business ethics with this system of business. This condition makes trading difficult because one party is always at a disadvantage in terms of trade between goods or services.

3. **Indivisibility of certain goods**

It is not possible to divide certain goods that will make exchange satisfactory to all. For example, a man wanting a horse for a sheep may demand more than four sheep for his horse BUT the other is not prepared to give four sheep and there can be no exchange.

4. **Difficulty in storing value**

Under the bartering system, it is difficult to store value. Perishable items like grains, fruits, etc. are expensive and difficult to store for long periods.

5. **Difficulty in making deferred payments**

In a barter economy, it is difficult to make payments in the future. Since payments are made in goods and services, debt contracts are not possible due to disagreements from both parties on the following grounds: It would often invite controversy as to the quality of the goods or services to be repaid.

History of subsistence economy to money economy

The subsistence economy has been in existence for ages before the introduction of money to acquire goods and services. It is a non-monetary economy which relied on natural resources to provide for basic needs, through hunting, gathering herbs, and wild fruits for food.

The exchange of goods and services worked well in the early stages of economic activity but with all the problems encountered with this exchange, money was introduced to make trading easier. Money reduced some of the problems that existed with bartering and opened the door for economic growth and development of societies.

Money

Money is anything that is used as a medium of exchange for goods and services. It is mostly in coins and banknotes. Money plays an important role in running a business.

Functions of money

1. **It serves as a medium of exchange** – Money can be used to purchase goods and services easily.
2. **A standard of deferred payments** – Goods and services can be priced, and customers given credit. For example, putting off payments for a later date such as a hire purchase.
3. **A unit of account** – Money makes it possible for units or prices to be given to goods and services, and their values are calculated.
4. **A store of value** – This means that money can be put away or saved.

Instruments of payments or exchange

This refers to the different ways that payments can be made for goods or services.

1. **Bills of exchange**

EXCHANGE FOR $60,000   3RD DECEMBER 2020

[STAMP]

85 days after date, pay Sherry or her order, a sum of dollars sixty thousand only for value received .....

To
Jerome & co.,
47, Trinidad.

Sherry Ali,
23, Tobago.

This is a binding agreement by one party (the drawee) to pay a fixed amount of cash to another party (the payee) within a predetermined date or on-demand. The drawer is the party that obliges the drawee to pay the payee. It is used mainly in international trade.

2. **Electronic transfer**

This is the transfer of funds from one account to another, either within a financial institution or across several institutions using computer systems. It can include moving funds from savings to checking, bill payments, or via credit card/debit card to pay for purchases.

3. **Telebanking**

This is a service provided by a bank or other financial institution. It simply enables the customers to perform different transactions over the telephone without the need to visit a bank branch or the Automated Teller Machine (ATM). Some examples of this include the movement of accounts, payment instructions (standing order).

4. **E-commerce (electronic commerce)**

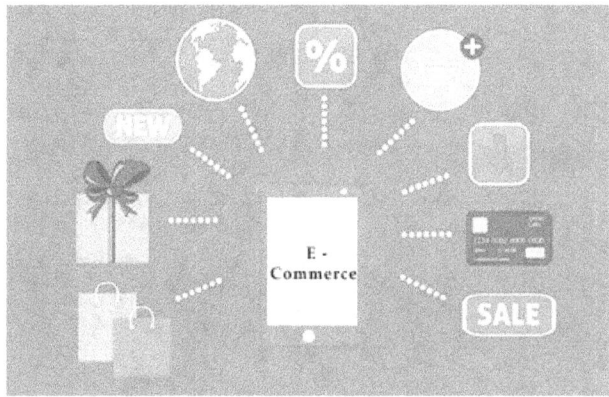

This is the activity of buying or selling of products using the Internet.

5. **Cheques**

A cheque is an order to pay a certain amount to a named person. The person authorizing payment is called the **drawer** and the person to whom payment is to be made is the **Payee.**

6. **Telegraphic money order**

This is a quick way of making payments or transferring sums of money to persons in local or overseas locations. It is a part of electronic banking.

7. **Credit card**

These are given by a financial institution to their customers. There is a limit on payments/purchases that can be made, and the amount used must be repaid by a date. Interest rates are charged on the amounts used.

8. **Debit card**

This is linked to the holder's savings account from which withdrawals, payments, or purchases are made. No interest is charged on withdrawal by the bank as there is an automatic deduction from the holder's account.

9. **Money order**

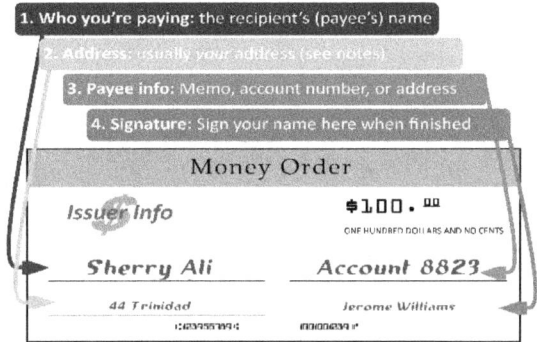

This is sold by a bank to persons who want to make overseas payments. It shows the amount of money to be paid to the person named in the order. It is given by the bank after the buyer has paid the amount as well as the bank fee.

10. **Bank draft**

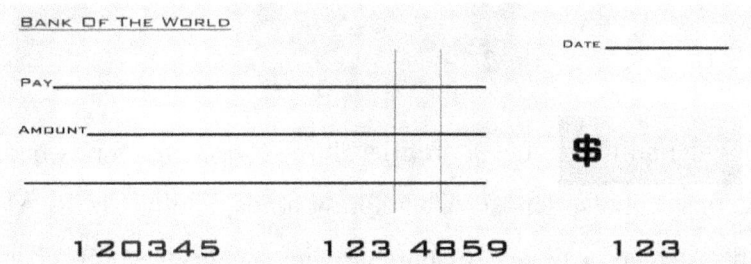

This is used when payments for goods or services are to be made in foreign currency. The person or business requiring the draft must pay the equivalent of the foreign currency needed. The bank charges a fee for this activity.

11. Bank transfers/credit transfer

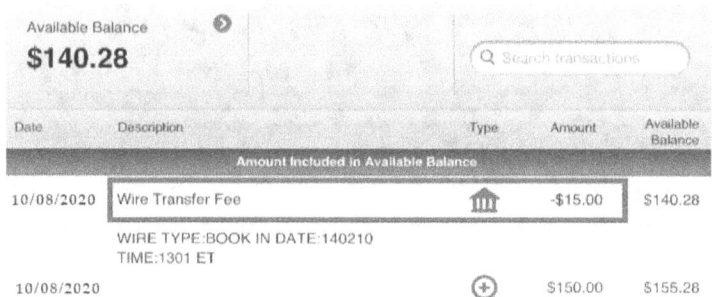

This is the transfer of money from one bank account to another electronically.

12. M-money (mobile money or mobile wallet)

This is the ability to use a **mobile phone** to transfer funds between banks or accounts, deposit or withdraw funds, and pay bills. Also, it can be used as a device to purchase items, whether physically or electronically.

Public and private sector

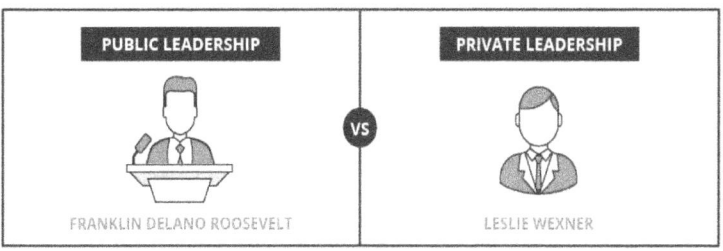

Public sector

This is the part of an economy that is controlled by the state (government). All activities in the public sector are for the benefit of all members of the society.

Private sector

This is that part of the economy that is owned and controlled by private individuals and firms.

Differences between public and private sectors

Category	Sector
1. Ownership and control	**Private sector** – Owned and controlled by private individuals, such as sole traders, partnerships, and private limited companies. **Public sector** – Owned and controlled by the government.

2. Objective	**Private sector** – Aims at making a profit. They are established to cater to the needs and wants of private individuals. **Public sector** – Aims at providing the basic and essential goods and services to the country and caters to the needs of its citizens.
3. Source of Capital	**Private sector** – The firms obtain capital from individuals who choose to buy shares in the enterprise. They also obtain capital from friends, family members, and personal savings or financial institutions such as credit unions or commercial banks. **Public sector** – Obtains funding from taxes, sale of oil and gas including loans from other governments or international banks.

Types of business structures

In business, there are different structures for its operation. These business structures include the proprietorship, partnership, corporation, and the limited liability company. Each business structure has its characteristics, advantages, and disadvantages as outlined below.

1. Sole trader/sole proprietor

In this business structure, one person owns and manages the business. He provides capital for the business and bears any losses or profits made.

Characteristics of a sole trader/sole proprietor
1. They are often small businesses
2. They are easy to establish and operate.
3. Very little capital is needed to start this type of business.

Advantages of a sole trader/sole proprietor
1. The owner enjoys all the profits of the business.
2. There is personal contact between the owner and the customers.
3. Decision making is both flexible and speedy.
4. The owner can work at his own pace.

5. The owner can explore more in versatility.

Disadvantages of a sole trader/sole proprietor
1. Long working hours especially at the beginning of the business.
2. Lack of continuity – if the owner dies, the business also dies.
3. Limited managerial skills – this can affect the quality of decisions.
4. Unlimited liability – this means that all losses and debts incurred by the business must be borne by the owner.
5. Lack of work-life balance – sole owners often find it hard to go on vacations since they have to look over the company.

Examples of sole trader businesses
Hairdressing/cosmetology services, grocery shops, small food service businesses, housecleaning services.

2. Partnership
This is a type of business operated by 2-20 persons for the common goal of making a profit.

Characteristics of a partnership business
1. Partners provide financial capital needed.
2. Profits/losses are shared between/among partners.
3. All partners bear the liability for the business' debts.

Partnerships are usually governed by an agreement/deed/contract. This will indicate:
1. How profits and losses will be shared.
2. If salaries are paid.
3. Procedures for admitting a new partner or what happens if a

partner dies or leaves the partnership or retires from the business.
4. The amount of capital each partner has invested.

If there is no partnership deed, the following will apply:
1. Profits/losses are shared equally.
2. No salaries are paid to partners.
3. No interest is paid on capital.
4. No interest is charged on drawings.

Advantages of a partnership business
1. More capital is available for the business.
2. There is greater borrowing capacity.
3. Workload can be shared among partners.
4. It is easy to establish.
5. Better decisions can be made (two good heads are better than one).

Disadvantages of a partnership business
1. Decisions may take longer to be made.
2. Owners have unlimited liability: This entails that all the partners are jointly as well as separately liable for the debt of the firm to an unlimited extent. They can share the liability among themselves and a member can be asked to settle all debts even from his personal properties.
3. Limited Capital: Since the total number of partners cannot exceed 20, the capital to be raised is always limited. Therefore, it may not be possible to start an exceptionally large business in partnership form.
4. Uncertainty of Life (lack of continuity): The partnership can

come to an end with the death, incapacity, or the retirement of any partner.

Types of partners

1. **Active partners** – These are the partners who actively participate in the daily activities and operation of a business. They contribute capital intending to share the profit and loss of the business. They are also liable for the debts of the firm.
2. **Silent partners** – These are the nonchalant partners who do not participate in the day-to-day activities of the partnership firm. They are known as dormant or sleeping partners. They only contribute capital and share the profits or bear the losses, if any.

3. Co-operatives(co-op)

This is a business that is owned, controlled, and operated by a group of users for their own benefit.

Characteristics of a co-operative

1. Membership is voluntary. Persons with common interests can become members of a co-operative. A member can also leave the organization by giving notice.
2. Members pool resources, for example, shares/capital for their benefit.
3. Members are also clients.
4. Members benefit from profits made.
5. Members exercise control and management by electing officers to run the organization.

Advantages of a co-operative
1. The members work together because they have the same needs and goals.
2. Decisions are made by all members.
3. Profit distribution (surplus earnings) to members is carried on in proportion to the use of service, the surplus may be allocated in shares or cash.
4. It has limited liability, that is, members are only responsible for the debts of the organization up to the amount invested.
5. It is owned and controlled by members.

Disadvantages of a co-operative
1. There is a longer decision-making process.
2. It requires all members to participate for success to be recorded.
3. Extensive record keeping is necessary in this form of organization.
4. Lack of managerial skills.
5. Access to limited capital.

Types of co-operatives
- ✓ Financial co-operative, for example, credit unions.
- ✓ Consumer co-operative involved in retail trade.
- ✓ Service co-operative – members are provided with a variety of services
- ✓ Agricultural/producers co-operative, for example, the cane farmers co-operatives, oil miner's co-operative

4. Franchises

This is a business that uses the name, logo, and trading systems of another successful business.

Characteristics of franchises
1. It is licensed by the parent company.
2. Pays a fee to the parent company.

Advantages of franchises
1. Franchises often have an existing reputation and image, proven management and work practices, and access to national advertising.
2. A franchise can be operated without any business experience. Franchisors usually provide the advice/training people need to operate their business model.
3. There is a higher tendency to succeed in a franchise than a start-up business.
4. It is easier to secure finance for a franchise. It is less expensive to buy a franchise than to start a personal business of the same type.

Disadvantages of franchises
1. Little room for creativity as a parent company determines how business is run.
2. Bad performances by other franchisees may affect one's franchise's reputation.
3. Buying a franchise means ongoing sharing of profit with the franchisor.
4. Franchisors do not have to renew an agreement at the end of the franchise term.

Examples of franchises

KFC, Burger King, McDonald's, etc.

N/B: Franchiser is the seller and Franchisee is the buyer.

5. Private and public companies

The comparison of public limited companies' and private limited companies

Item of comparison	Public limited company	Private limited company
Meaning	A public company is a company that is owned and operated publicly.	A private company is a company that is owned and operated privately.
Minimum members	7	2
Maximum members	Unlimited	50

Private limited company

Characteristics of a private company

1. Shareholders enjoy limited liability, that is, in the event of bankruptcy, they stand to lose only their investment and not their personal assets.
2. They are financed through funds of private individuals, financial institutions, retained profits, etc.
3. The company must be registered with the Registrar of Companies.
4. They must include the term 'limited'(Ltd) as part of their name.

5. There is a minimum of 2 and a maximum of 50 shareholders.
6. Their shares cannot be traded on the Stock Exchange.
7. These firms have unlimited life in that they continue after the death of a shareholder or shareholders.

Advantages of a private limited company
1. Shareholders have limited liability.
2. It is easy to obtain loans for expansion, etc.
3. The company has a lifetime existence until and unless it is liquidated.

Disadvantages of a private company
1. Restricted number of shareholders.
2. Annual financial reports must be submitted to the Registrar of Companies.
3. Shares are not transferable without the directors' consent.
4. The amount of capital is limited, and growth is slow.

Public limited company

Characteristics of a public company
1. There must be at least seven shareholders.
2. Capital/finance can be obtained from shareholders or borrowing from banks and other financial institutions.
3. Shares are traded on the stock market.
4. Members of the company have limited liability.
5. A board of directors is elected to control the decision making of the business.

Advantages of a public company
1. Shareholders have limited liability.
2. Large amounts of capital can be raised.

3. The company can grow and obtain economies of scale.

Disadvantages of a public company
1. They can lose touch with their customers and workers because of their size.
2. They are more difficult to manage.
3. The legal requirements to operate may be costly and time-consuming.
4. Annual financial reports must be made public.

Formation of a public limited company

The documents in setting up a company are:

Memorandum of association - This includes the following:
1. Name of company.
2. Address of the company.
3. Objectives/mission statement of the company.
4. Amount of capital & number and types of shares.

Articles of association - This document sets out the constitution or internal rules and regulations of the proposed business. It includes the following:
1. Names of directors and their duties.
2. Voting procedures.
3. Rules governing meetings.
4. How profits will be shared.
5. Rights of shareholders and classes of shareholders.

Prospectus – This is a document that invites the public to buy shares. It gives investors detailed information about the shares.

Economic systems

The economic system refers to an organized manner in which a country allocates resources and distributes goods and services across the whole nation or a given geographic area. The different types, characteristics, advantages, and disadvantages are explained below.

Types of economic systems

1. **Traditional (subsistence)**

In this type of Economic system, the needs and wants are provided by direct production (for example, fishing, hunting, and planting). Little surplus is produced and there is no government involvement.

2. **Command/planned economic system**

In this system, the government owns and controls the production in a country. Examples of countries that practice this system include Cuba, Venezuela, etc.

Characteristics of economic systems

1. The government owns and runs factories, transportation systems, etc.
2. They also decide what and how much to produce.
3. Prices are set by the government.
4. The government plans, controls, and coordinates all economic activities.

Advantages of economic systems

1. No group of workers can influence the prices of goods or their salaries.
2. Income is more evenly distributed.
3. Competition is avoided.
4. There is a greater emphasis on quality of life (health,

education, etc.) than on the quantity of production.
5. The exact demands of a society can be met, reducing waste.

Disadvantages of economic systems
1. Wages may be low.
2. No freedom of choice for consumers or producers due to lack of competition.
3. It limits the innovation/creativity of workers.
4. It encourages illegal activities of a business. For example, the black market/underground market flourishes so that goods or services needed can be received without any restrictions from the government.

Free Enterprise/Capitalist or Market Economy

In this system of business, private individuals make their own choices on how resources will be used. There is no government control. Some examples of countries that apply this system are the USA and England.

Characteristics of free enterprise
1. Consumer's choice determines what is produced.
2. The factors of production (land, labour, and capital) are owned and controlled by private individuals rather than the government.
3. Limited government control.
4. Most economic decisions are made by buyers and sellers, not the government.

Advantages of free enterprise
1. The consumer can choose to buy from the variety of goods

that are produced.
2. Competition among firms can reduce the prices of goods or services.
3. Goods demanded by the consumer are produced and goods that are not demanded are suspended.
4. It can easily adapt to sudden changes in the demand for a product or service.
5. There is a lack of government intervention.

Disadvantages of free enterprise
1. Only goods that yield the highest profits will be produced.
2. Consumers can be exploited through high prices for essential services if there is limited competition for the provision of these goods/services.
3. It leads to inequalities of wealth, this entails that the rich get richer and the poor get poorer.
4. Consumers can buy goods that are not so good for them, for example, cigarettes and alcohol, illegal drugs (DEMERIT GOODS) at the expense of goods/services which are important, for instance, dental care, health care, fruit and vegetables, and fitness memberships (MERIT GOODS).

Mixed economy or dual economy

This refers to where resources are controlled by both private individuals and the government. This system is practiced by some countries like Trinidad and Tobago, and Barbados.

Characteristics of mixed economy
1. BOTH the government and private sector make decisions on what to produce, how to produce, and for whom to produce.

2. Consumers may be protected from exploitation by the establishment of consumer bodies.

Advantages of mixed economy
1. The government can protect consumers from unfair trading practices by passing laws.
2. Both government and private sectors can cooperate in the delivery of essential services such as transport, education, health, etc.
3. It provides the freedom to own private property.
4. It promotes a quick economic development.

Disadvantages of mixed economy
1. It brings about the fear of nationalization. As the private sector and public-sector work together, the government would have the ability to own and nationalize any industry.
2. It can lead to higher taxes.
3. Delays in economic decisions.
4. More wastage.

Functional areas of a business

The functional areas of a business are the production, marketing and sales, finance, personnel or human resources, research, and development.

Production

The production function of the business involves transforming raw materials into finished products to satisfy customers' needs and wants. Production function may include the following:
1. The purchase of raw materials.
2. Making the product.

3. Storage of finished goods.
4. Maintaining proper inventory (stock) management.

Finance/accounting

This department is responsible for maintaining a good cash flow (income & expenditure), payment of wages and salaries, payment to suppliers, and producing the business' financial statements.

Personnel/HR function

This department is responsible for recruiting, training, disciplining staff, and handling staff welfare.

Marketing

This department is responsible for finding out what customers want. It includes market research, designing products, pricing, and advertising.

Research and development

This department is responsible for creating new designs and styles as well as search for new ways to produce their products using the latest technology.

Stakeholders of a business

A stakeholder is any person, group of people, or organization that has an interest in the business.

Stakeholders	Role
Customers	Provide feedback to the business about products. Purchase goods and services that allow the business to make a profit.

Suppliers	Supply quality goods and services to the business at an affordable cost. Deliver goods on time.
Employees	Perform their duties well according to their job description. Use business' resources efficiently.
Government	They offer assistance to businesses, for example, giving loans, training, and proper infrastructure. Protect customers from exploitation. Collect taxes from businesses.
Employers	To provide quality goods and services To provide jobs to the community.
Community	To safeguard the environment from pollution. Provide persons seeking employment.
Bankers	Ensures that loans are repaid in

	a timely manner.

Legal & ethical issues in operating a business

Legal issues – This refers to the business abiding by the laws of the country.

Ethical issues – This refers to the moral (right or wrong) conduct of the business. For a business to operate legally and ethically the following factors could be put into consideration.

Code of ethics

This is a guide to help workers conduct business transparently and with integrity. It shows the mission and standards of the business. It is incorporated in the Business Ethics, for example, the Hippocratic oath in medical ethics.

Environmental policy

This is any measure by business to prevent or reduce the effects of its operations on the environment. This includes the proper disposal of waste and reducing effects on pollution such as air pollution.

Handling of personal information

Employee records should be treated with confidence. In other words, there should be non-disclosure of the data and information to anyone within or outside of the organization.

Negative effects of unethical and illegal practices on a business

- ✓ **Misleading advertisements** – This comprises the unfair and fraudulent practices on the population.
- ✓ **Withholding of tax** – This refers to cheating the government of revenue, which affecting economic development.
- ✓ **Unethical disposal of waste** – This refers to the improper

disposal of waste which could lead to pollution and poor health issues.
- ✓ **Money laundering** – This is the process of making illegally-gained proceeds (fondly called "dirty money") appear legal. It reduces government tax revenue and makes government tax collection more difficult.

Careers in business

Software developer

The software developers are computer programmers who design, build, and test computer programmes for businesses. They create and maintain computer programs through coding. They are the creative masterminds behind the software and systems to run devices and computer-related tasks.

Web designer

A web designer is responsible for creating the design and layout of a website or web pages by combining text with sounds, pictures, graphics, and video clips.

Compliance officers

A compliance officer ensures that the business operates with accepted standards, laws, and policies both internally and externally.

Information officers

The information officers are government or business employees that are responsible for creating and enabling communication between the government/business organization, the news media, and the public. They provide information about activities, plans, etc. to the public and media.

Strategic planners

The strategic planners ensure the development of business plans to realize their objectives, for example, growth and profitability. They also help the business maintain its competitive advantage and allocate resources appropriately.

Advertising/public relations.

This involves building positive relationships with stakeholders, media, and the public through newspapers, radio shows, television, etc. The aim is to inform the public about the business' products.

Web planners

The web planners are a versatile team who plans and manage the staff, resources, budget, and other administrative supports of the web team.

Entrepreneur

This is a person who brings his unique idea to start a business. He organizes, manages, and assumes the risks of that business or enterprise.

UNIT 2
INTERNAL ORGANIZATIONAL ENVIRONMENT

Management

Management is the bringing together of all resources (labour, land, capital, skills) to meet the goals of an organization.

Functions of management

1. **Planning** – This is concerned with defining goals for future performance and deciding on what tasks and resources that will be needed.
2. **Organizing** – This the process of putting together all resources needed to meet the goals of the organization.
3. **Directing** – This is the process by which actual performance is guided towards the goals to be met.
4. **Controlling** – This is the process of checking how activities are being carried out in the business.
5. **Coordinating** – Bringing other management functions so that the business performs efficiently.

6. **Delegating** – Entails assigning duties to the lower-level employees and granting them the necessary authority to carry out such duties.
7. **Motivating** – This is where workers are encouraged to take the right actions to get their job done.

Ways managers motivate employees

1. **Promotion** – This is the activity of upgrading the employees from a lower to a higher level. It is a good way of rewarding and motivating the employees for it boosts the employees' productivity. Most times, promotion attracts an increase in salary.
2. **Increase in salary** – A manager can greatly motivate his employees by increasing their salaries. An increment of salary can lead to additional work input from the employees.
3. **Back pay** – This refers to the money and benefits to which an employee is granted for a past work or a retroactive pay increase. This is a good way to motivate employees.
4. **Good working conditions** – The provision of a good and favourable working environment by the manager practically motivates the employees as it enables them to work with great comfortability.

Responsibilities of Management

1. **Responsibilities of management to owners/shareholders of a company**
   a. Achieving the highest profit level.
   b. Maximizes the efficient use of resources.
   c. Ensuring the growth and development of the firm.

d. Providing information.

2. **Responsibilities of management to employees**
   a. Paying fair wages.
   b. Protection against unfair discrimination.
   c. Protecting the health and safety of employees.
   d. Providing compensation for job-related injuries.

3. **Responsibilities of management to customers**
   a. Providing high-quality goods and services at a reasonable price.
   b. Providing good after-sale services such as transportation, warranty, and delivery.
   c. Carrying out fair trading practices.
   d. Timely delivery of orders made.

4. **Responsibilities of management to society**
   a. Avoids pollution of the environment.
   b. Conserves scarce resources.
   c. Preserves local culture and tradition.
   d. Supports charitable organizations.

5. **Responsibilities of management to government**
   a. Abides by the laws of the land.
   b. Pays corporation tax when due.
   c. Makes deductions from employees' salaries such as national insurance and income tax.

Organizational chart

An organizational chart is a diagram of an organization structure, showing the levels of management hierarchy and the formal lines of responsibility.

Purpose of organizational chart

- It shows the division of the labour force in the business.
- It shows who controls the labour force.
- It shows who has the authority and responsibility.

Components of an organizational chart

1. Line organization

This is a form of organization where the lines of authority are direct. There is a chain of command, which means that each subordinate knows from where they take orders. Authority flows from the top of the organization to the bottom.

Chain of command – This is the way authority flows from the top of the organization to the employees at the lower levels. It shows the hierarchy of employees.

Span of control – This is the number of employees that is controlled by a manager in a department.

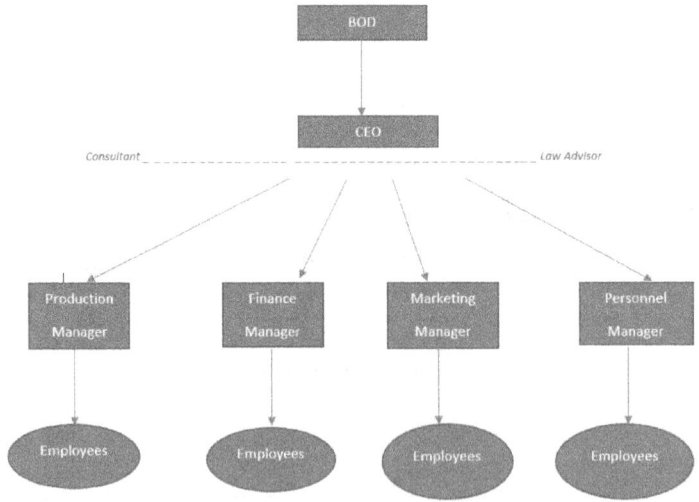

Figure 1, showing a simple organization chart

2. Staff organization

This is the organization of staff managers who provide personal assistance to a senior manager or is an advisor on a matter. For example, an advertising expert could provide some technical information, advice, or opinion to the marketing manager to develop a sales strategy for a new product.

Staff managers have **no authority** over line workers in a department, they only provide **advice** on matters.

Benefits of staff managers

1. They provide a service for which the whole organization benefits from their expertise.
2. Expert advice is given to line managers which helps to improve overall business performance.

3. Functional relationships

A functional relationship exists when a specialist manager is responsible for a specific function within several departments. For example, a cost accountant may be responsible for the costing of all jobs in a business.

Benefits of functional relationships

1. Expert advice is available at any time.
2. Versatile in spurring innovative ideas.

Disadvantages of functional relationships

1. Employees may have more than one supervisor.
2. There may be conflicts between managers.

Leadership

This is the ability to motivate, influence, and direct the performance of workers towards achieving a common goal.

Characteristics of a good leader

1. Honesty
2. Flexibility
3. Focus
4. Ability to make intelligent decisions.
5. Takes risks.
6. Creative and innovative.

Leadership styles

Autocratic/Authoritarian style

An autocratic leader assumes responsibility for all decisions made and does not allow others to make an input.

Advantages of autocratic style

1. The leader makes all decisions timely.
2. The leader supervises work closely.
3. There is a fast-one-way communication with workers.

Disadvantages of autocratic style

1. It demotivates workers who want to contribute and accept responsibility.
2. It gives little information to workers.
3. Decisions do not benefit from workers knowledge and experience.

Democratic/participative style

This leader allows workers to participate in decision making at all levels in the organization.

Advantages of democratic style

1. Workers are involved in decision making which can lead to better decisions.
2. There is a two-way communication that allows feedback from workers.

Disadvantages of democratic style

1. Consultations with the staff can be time-consuming.
2. On some occasions, quick decisions without the input of workers will be needed.

Laissez-faire style

This leader sets goals for subordinates and then leaves them alone to achieve these goals. This style works well when workers are willing and able to accept responsibility.

Advantages of laissez-faire style

1. There is little management supervision which can motivate some workers.
2. It gives room for independency, exposition, and exploration of new ideas/thoughts.
3. It boosts the employees' leadership skills.

Disadvantages of laissez-faire style

1. Not effective if the manager cannot control workers when it is needed.
2. The employees can abuse the advantage of not being supervised always.

3. It could lead to poor responsibility and accountability.

Internal source of conflict

In this context, conflict means the disagreement between managers and workers which can cause serious problems if not resolved.

The sources of conflict

- ✓ Employees roles not clearly defined.
- ✓ Workers paid low salaries.
- ✓ Employees not working as a team.
- ✓ Communications with workers if not clear.

Trade union

This is a group of workers who are employed in an industry, that come together to improve their wages and working conditions.

Functions of a trade union

1. To get better working conditions for employees.
2. To obtain higher wages for workers.
3. To settle disputes between members and the employer.
4. To ensure that workers have job security.

Employers strategies to gain upper hand during a conflict

1. Lockout – This is where employees are told to stay at home as the business is closed.
2. Dismissing all workers who are on strike.
3. Using scab labour – These are temporary workers who are hired to work during the strike.

Employees strategies to gain upper hand during a conflict

1. **Picketing** – Employees gathering at the entrance of the business and tries to influence other workers to stay away from work.

2. **Strike action** – The union can organize for workers to stop work during a period.
3. **Work to rule** – Workers perform only the duties required in their job, no overtime or additional duties are done.
4. **Go-slow** – This is where workers deliberately work at a slow pace without breaking any company rules.
5. **Sick out** – This is where workers plan to take a deliberate sick leave without being sick.

Strategies for handling conflict within an organization

1. **Mediation** – This involves the third-party prosing solutions to problems which are considered. The third-party cannot force acceptance of any suggestions.
2. **Arbitration** – The two parties agree to ask the third party to give the solution, which they both must accept. Therefore, the agreement is legally binding on both parties.
3. **Conciliation** – A third party will be present during discussions with both parties and encourage the parties to reach an agreement.

Settlement of disputes or grievance procedure

1. The union representative is notified by workers of a dispute.
2. The union representative takes up the matter with the supervisor or manager.
3. If the matter is unresolved, the union representative will report to the office of the trade union.
4. The union office will then hold talks with the senior manager of the firm.

5. If this fails, the union representative will report to the union executive.
6. An executive member of the union will hold talks with the manager of the division.
7. If this fails, the management of the business will inform the Chief Labour officer that a dispute exists. The Chief Labour Officer would then try to get all parties to agree.

Guidelines for establishing a good relationship between managers and employees

Strategies for motivating employees
- ✓ Proper communication between management and employees.
- ✓ Motivation of employees.
- ✓ Employees having job security.
- ✓ Employees having good working conditions.
- ✓ Management practicing a good leadership style.
- ✓ Management displaying a sense of fairness to all employees.

Teamwork

Teamwork is the activity where two or more persons come together to work and achieve a common goal. There are some advantages and disadvantages of Teamwork.

Advantages of teamwork
1. It improves the working relationship among workers.
2. It increases communication among persons.
3. It improves business performance.
4. It increases cooperation among members.
5. Skills and knowledge can be passed on from one person to another.

Disadvantages of Teamwork

1. Disagreement can be time-consuming.
2. Some workers may let others do their work.
3. Conflict can exist which can negatively affect business goals.
4. Differences in personality can lead to clashes.

Communication

The is the exchange of information between two persons. It is made up of a sender, a message, the medium, a receiver, and feedback.

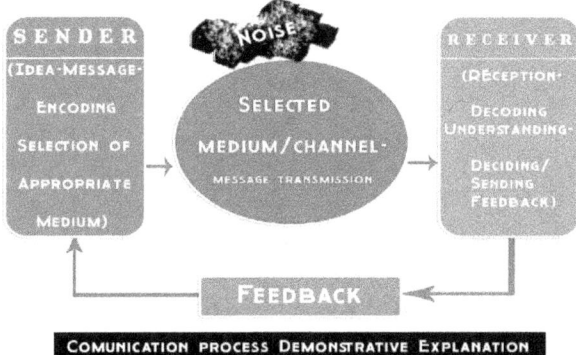

Strategies for Effective Communication Between Persons

- ✓ The message must be clear.
- ✓ The message should be concise (short).
- ✓ The message should be comprehensive and correct.
- ✓ The message should be able to influence the receiver to give feedback.

UNIT 3
ESTABLISHING A BUSINESS

Establishing a business is not always as easy as it may sound. It takes a lot of sensitive questions and factors to be considered to establish, run, and operate a business successfully. These factors range from the type of business to be established, the business idea and plan, the best geographical location, acquisition of a great communicative skill, a good knowledge of the business strategy, capital and finance, and a lot more. Above all, to establish a business successfully, one ought to possess the qualities of a good entrepreneur.

An entrepreneur

An Entrepreneur is a person who undertakes the risk of investing to create and market goods and services for a profit.

Function of an entrepreneur
- ✓ **Conceptualization** – This is where new business goals or ideas and generated by the entrepreneur.
- ✓ **Planning** – When goals are created, ways of accomplishing

them must be identified by the entrepreneur.
- ✓ **Accessing funds** – This is where the entrepreneur finds ways to finance the business. For example, by taking loans or from their savings.
- ✓ **Organizing the business** – Keeping records and documentation, creating a formal structure with activities, and having authority assigned to different persons.
- ✓ **Operating and evaluating the business performance** – Ensuring that the day-to-day activities are carried out and reviewing performance over some time.
- ✓ **Risk bearing** – The entrepreneur will make risky decisions, to make profits.

Personal traits and leadership qualities of an entrepreneur

- ✓ **Flexibility** - The ability to make changes quickly when a situation occurs in the business.
- ✓ **Creativity** – This is the ability to develop ideas or new ways of doing things and satisfying customer needs.
- ✓ **Innovative** – Creating a new idea to replace an existing one.
- ✓ **Goal-oriented** – Entrepreneurs must set goals to get the level of success they desire.
- ✓ **Takes calculated risk** – An entrepreneur must be willing to take personal risks to make a profit.
- ✓ **Organize** – They must keep the necessary documents as proof of what transactions occurred and determine what resources are needed for the efficient operation of the business.

Ways entrepreneurs contribute to economic development
1. They create employment for persons living in the country.
2. They provide goods and services to satisfy customers' needs.
3. They purchase local materials that provide income for other businesses.
4. They help earn foreign currency when goods are sold abroad to other countries.

Steps taken to establish a business
1. **Conceptualization** – A business always begins when a new product or service is to be offered. This is simply called conceptualization.
2. **Research** – The entrepreneur makes an investment and takes all the risks when a new business is started. Research must first be done to see if the business idea is a profitable and lucrative one. This helps to minimize possible losses.
3. **Identification of resources** – Once the business is a favourable one, entrepreneurs must decide what resources are needed to operate the business. Resources include capital and human row resources.
4. **Creation of a business plan** – A document that provides information on the resources, activities to be done in the business, and how customers' needs will be met.
5. **Acquisition of funds** – These are the ways that capital will be raised to start the business. This includes owners saving, loans from banks, and money borrowed from family and friends.
6. **Operations of the business** – The entrepreneur will become

the manager of the business by running the day-to-day operations.

Reasons for starting a business

There are many reasons behind the establishment of every business. They are as follows:

1. **Financial independence** – An entrepreneur starts a business to work for themselves. The idea of becoming a self-boss is the main reason for starting a new business.
2. **Self-fulfilment** – When an individual starts a personal business, he/she feels a sense of accomplishment. This sense of accomplishment carries a feeling that they are doing what truly matters to them in life.
3. **Increased income** – As a business owner, all profits go to the owner. This creates more income for the entrepreneur which leads to greater wealth and a higher standard of living.
4. **Control of working life** – As an entrepreneur, you can decide when and where you will work. This gives the owner a level of flexibility. Although an entrepreneur works hard, they have control of how they do it

Difference between entrepreneur and entrepreneurship

An Entrepreneur refers to a person who organizes, manages, and operates multiple businesses with different goals and takes financial risks.

Entrepreneurship is defined as the process of starting, executing business activities with various departments in the business.

Business plan

A Business plan is a document that provides information on the resources, activities to be done in the business, and how customers' needs will be met.

Elements in a business plan

1. **Executive summary** – This is the first part of a business plan, but it is usually done last. It summarizes all the necessary points of the proposed business. This includes the name of the business, the type of business, and its objectives.
2. **The operational plan** – This is information about the business and its objectives. It includes:
   a. The name of business.
   b. Address of business.
   c. The objectives of the business.
   d. The legal structure of the business.
   e. Who will be its suppliers?
   f. Equipment needed for the business.
   g. The staff required for the business.
3. **Identify the business opportunity** – This describes the goods or services that will be offered to the customers.
4. **The marketing plan** – This identifies the potential customers of the business, product strategies, and pricing strategies.
5. **Financial forecast** – This includes where the capital will be raised, the projected sales for the business, the estimated cash flow, and projected profits for the business.

Reasons for preparing a business plan

1. To attract potential investors to the business idea, to gain the funding needed to start or expand the business.
2. To be a guide in running the day-to-day operation of the business based on the goals established.
3. To ensure that sufficient research is conducted into the viability of the business idea to be profitable.
4. To be used as a blueprint for securing finance from any financial institution such as a bank.

Market research

Market research is the process of collecting and analyzing data by an entrepreneur in order to make decisions in the business.

Types of market research

1. **Primary research**

This is research that was collected for the first time or first-hand. It is new and was done to answer a specific issue in the business. Primary research comes from customer surveys (questionnaires).

2. **Secondary research**

This is research that was collected for an issue in the past, it is information that was already available.

Secondary research comes from the internet, the company published financial records on the newspapers, government offices such as the Central Statistical Office and magazines or books.

Feasibility study

Feasibility study is a detailed assessment and research of the practicality of a business idea to ensure its feasibility. It looks at the market demand for the product or service, the potential customers for the product, the methods to be used in producing the product, and what profits will be made.

Benefits of a feasibility study

1. It determines where capital will be raised for the business, (loans, savings, investors).
2. It assists to know if the business idea is a good one.
3. It helps with decision-making about the cost of the business.
4. Provides documentation that the business idea was investigated.

Planning

Planning is the process of the entrepreneur setting goals to be achieved by the business within a certain time.

Types of planning

1. **Short-term planning**

These are goals that are set for the next one to three years within the business. These plans are made by supervisors and other lower-level employees. This guides the day-to-day running of the business.

2. **Medium-term planning**

These are goals that are set for the next three to ten years These plans are made by middle-level managers on what their departments should achieve within the specified time.

3. **Long-term planning**

These are usually prepared for the next ten years in the future of the business. These are made by directors or top management within the business. It covers major decisions and plans for the business.

Collateral

Collateral refers to the assets that belong to the borrower for which the lender can sell if the borrower cannot pay back the loan given, at the agreed time.

Types of collateral

1. **Property** – This can be in the form of land and building for which the borrower uses as security to get the loan.
2. **Bonds** – These are certificates that represent money to be paid at a later date. The payment of the bond can be used as the collateral to secure the loan.
3. **Money** – These are liquid assets in the form of cash that can be used to secure the loan as a down payment.
4. **Cash surrender insurance policies** – Life insurance that carries a cash value can also be used as a collateral to secure a loan.
5. **Motor vehicle** – Depending on the brand of the vehicle, good ones can be used as the asset to secure the loan.

NOTE: All of the above items, when used as collateral, carry along the idea that if the borrower cannot repay their loan, the lender will have all rights to sell the assets in order to recover the loan given. This is the essence of collateral.

Ways the government can regulate businesses
1. The establishment of institutions such as the Bureau of Standards which are responsible for maintaining the quality and contents of certain products.
2. The granting of licenses – Businesses must meet certain requirements for licenses to be granted. For example, getting a bar license, license for the sale of drugs, and a food badge license.
3. The charging of taxes – This forces the business to pay some of its profits to the government.
4. Location – The government can locate businesses in a certain area. For example, the Omera Industrial estate and Macoya Industrial estate.

Factors affecting the location of a business

1. **Geographical factors**

Some businesses will choose to locate in areas that have certain features. For example, a hotel will locate near beaches and shipping companies near seaports.

2. **Labour supply and cost**

Businesses will choose to locate where there is an available supply of workers at a reasonable cost. The business needs to have enough workers to run its operation. Labour costs can affect the firm's ability to make a profit.

3. **Transport cost**

A business that uses heavy and bulky raw materials will locate to its supplier. This will reduce the cost of transporting the raw materials to the business.

4. **Power and water**

Reliable power supply and access to clean water will influence where a business locates. The cost of these factors will also impact a firm's decision to locate in a country.

5. **Government regulations**

Governments can use grants and tax breaks to motivate businesses to locate in a specific area.

6. **Health facilities**

Good health facilities help to keep a workforce healthy and capable of working. Therefore, managers will prefer to locate in countries where there are good health facilities.

7. **Infrastructure**

The quality of local roads, transportation, and technology links will influence where businesses locate. For example, the poor quality of internet connection can negatively affect a business operation.

8. **Site cost**

The cost of purchasing property or a building can be expensive in some areas. Businesses will, therefore, must determine what cost they are willing to pay based on their budget.

UNIT 4
LEGAL ASPECTS OF A BUSINESS

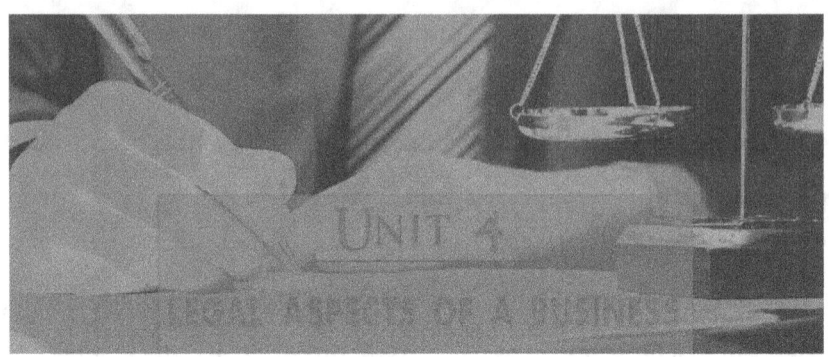

To establish a business, it is always a good habit to consider the legal aspects of the business. This activity does not only expose one to some legal knowledge about the business but also give necessary legal backups and safeguard the business from any legal issues. The legal factors to be considered are explained below.

Contract

A contract is a legally binding agreement between two or more persons that is enforced by law.

Features of a contract

1. **Offer** – An offer is a proposal by one party to enter a contract. The person making the offer is the **offeror** and the person the offer is made to is the **offeree**. An offer can be oral, written, or implied. An offer can be made to a specific person or the public.

2. **Acceptance** – This is where the **offeree** willingly agrees to accept the terms of the offer made by the other party(**offeror**), without conditions.

3. **Consideration** – This refers to **what is exchanged** between the two parties to ensure that there is a contract. This bargain for exchange must feature a legal determinant to the promisor or a legal benefit to the promise. In most cases, it represents the price paid and must be lawful, real, viable, and present.
4. **Capacity** – This is the **legal capability** to form a binding contract. Some people cannot enter a contract such as minors, the mentally challenged/deranged, those under the influence of drugs/alcohol, persons who have a physical disability, for example, the blind or deaf people.

Types of contracts

1. **Simple contract**

A **simple contract** is a contract made in **written** or **oral** method, rather than a contract made under seal. **Simple contracts** require **consideration** to be valid. **Simple contracts** may be implied from the conduct of parties bound by the contract. Examples of simple contracts: The Purchase of Goods, Transportation, and the Supply of services

2. **Specialty contracts**

A **specialty contract** is an official type of contract that is **written**, compulsorily **signed**, **sealed**, and **delivered**. They are also referred to as **contracts by deed** or **contracts under seal**. Examples of specialty contracts: Mortgages, Sale of land, Insurance, and Hire purchase.

Rules governing offer & acceptance

1. An offer must be communicated to the other party. An offer can be made to a specific person or the public. However,

acceptance must be made by some specific person/persons.
2. An offer lost in the post cannot be regarded as an offer since it has not reached its destination.
3. Acceptance must be unconditional, for example, an offer must be accepted as it is. Therefore, a counteroffer made must be accepted by both parties before a contract can exist.
4. Acceptance must be within an agreed time.

Ways of terminating contracts

1. **Performance** – Both parties **carried out** their side of the agreement.
2. **Agreement** – Both parties **agree to cancel** the contract before it is completed.
3. **Breach** – One party breaks the contract by failing to carry out his side of the agreement.
4. **Impossibility** – One party is unable to meet their obligations because of **circumstances beyond their control**. For example, change in law preventing the exportation of a specific product.
5. **Lapse of time** – This is where the intended recipient (offeree) does not respond to the offer within the **time** stipulated or in a **reasonable time**. An offer to a **contract** cannot remain open indefinitely, so it is usually only valid for a prescribed period.
6. **Death** – This is where one party dies before the contract was completed.

Valid & void/invalid contracts

Valid contracts – These are contracts with all the required elements of a valid contract. It is valid and enforceable in a court of law.

Example of a valid contract

A moral agent signed a contract with the appliance store to buy a refrigerator, paid for the refrigerator and the appliance store delivered the product safely.

Void/invalid contracts – These are illegal contracts. They have no effect and are not enforceable in a court of law. Most commonly, a void contract lacks one or all the essential elements needed for it to be valid. Since it is not a valid contract, neither party needs to act and to terminate it.

Example of a void contract

A contract between an illegal drug dealer and an illegal drug supplier to purchase a specified quantity of drugs for a specified amount. Either one of the parties could void the contract since it is missing one of the elements of a valid contract.

Circumstances under which a contract may be rendered void/invalid

- An agreement between a client and owner of a brothel whose services satisfy the basic elements of a contract for services will be deemed to be invalid since prostitution in most countries is an illegal act.
- If it can be proven that one of the parties was subject to duress when entering the contract, then the contract may be rendered invalid. It is assumed that the parties to contracts are free moral agents and are acting of their own free will

without any form of coercion. Any contract entered which can be shown to lack these conditions will be rendered invalid.

- A contract that involves some action that is against society's values or which goes against the "public good" would be deemed to be unenforceable and invalid. For example, in countries where the possession and use of marijuana is unlawful, attempting to bind a party to a contract to supply marijuana would be an unlawful contract and make that contract invalid.

Importance of record-keeping in a business

In running a business, it is a good habit to keep good records of every activity of the business. Record-keeping, therefore, is of utmost necessity as it helps one to achieve the following:

1. Monitoring and evaluation of business progress

To monitor the business progress, one needs good records of the business activities. Good business records can statistically show the improvement of a business, the nature of a business, the daily/monthly sales, profit and loss, the business status quo, as well as the subsequent changes to ensure the success of the business.

2. Preparation for financial statements

Good business records are truly relevant in order to prepare accurate financial statements of the business. These include income (profit and loss) statements and balance sheets. These statements play a major role in dealing with the bank, creditors, and in the management of every business.

3. Proper identification of the sources of income

In every business, there are many sources of receiving money or property. These different sources of income are incorporated in the business record to be easily identified at any given time. Therefore, a good business record helps one to separate business from non-business receipts, and taxable from non-taxable income when operating a business.

4. Keeping track of the deductible expenses

In operating a business, some expenses are very spontaneous, and the inability to keep a record of them would lead to poor accountability. Such a simple mistake could ruin a business gradually.

5. Preparation of the tax return

Keeping a good business record is of utmost necessity because it aids one to prepare the tax returns of the business. Also, these records must support the income and expenses of the business.

6. Support items reported on tax returns

A good business record prepares one for inspection by the tax agency. If required, the business may have to explain the items reported.

Business documents

Business documents are all the records, books, files, presentations, reports, and documentation of all kinds concerning a business. They could be in paper (written), electronic, or any type of format. The business documents are as follows:

1. **Letter of inquiry**

   Hi, I write to inquire from some trusted sources of your possession of some highly responsive WordPress Plugins and would very much like to learn more about it. I would really appreciate if you can send any information about some signature plugins to help me in my selection process. Please, kindly incorporate the unique features, prices, discounts, warrannty , and vip support.

   Please, if you need to know more about my requirements, or if you have further questions, kindly reach out to me as I look forward to hearing from you soon.

   Best regards,
   Pereere.

This is the document sent by a person who wishes to know about the goods and services a business has to offer (price, description, etc.).

2. **Quotation**

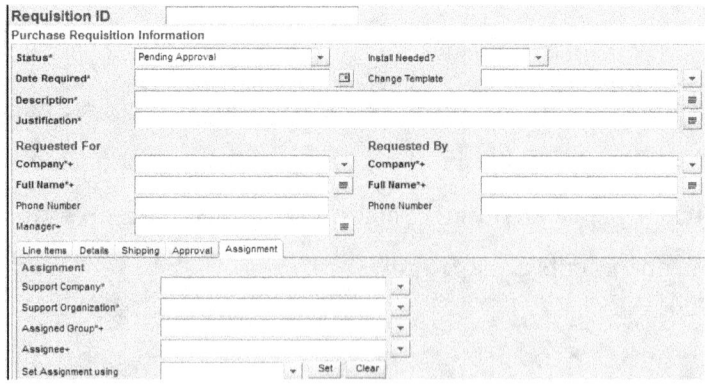

This is a document that lists the prices of all items in stock.

3. **Order/purchase requisition**

This is a document requesting a certain quantity of goods at a specific time.

4. Delivery note

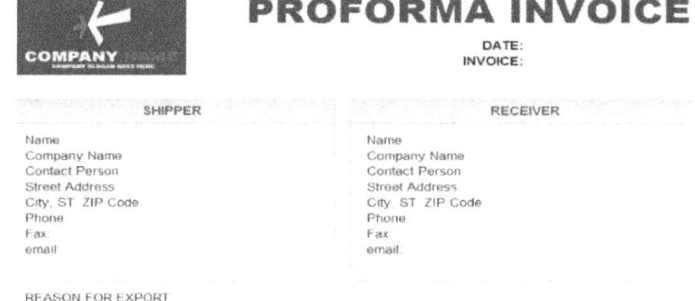

This is a document signed upon the delivery of items to the purchaser. It provides proof of the delivery of goods.

5. Proforma invoice

This is a preliminary bill of sale sent by a supplier at the request of a prospective buyer. It outlines a seller's intent to deliver products or services to customers for a specific price. As the price has not been agreed yet, it is not a real invoice. If the customer is interested, an actual invoice is sent. It is used when the purchaser's creditworthiness is unknown by the supplier.

6. Invoice

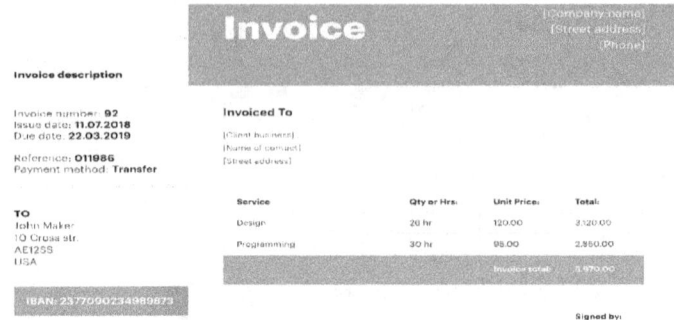

This is known as a bill and is sent by the supplier to the purchaser giving details of the purchase. It must show the quantity of each item bought with its price.

7. Statement of accounts

This is sent by the creditor/seller to the debtor/purchaser showing a record of transactions between them, that is, the goods supplied, what is owed and the payments made.

8. Stock card

Stock Card

Stock item: Sony 30cm colour TV				Product code: STV84920030					
Supplier: Wholesale Electricals				Location: West 15					
				Valuation method: FIFO					

Date	Reference	IN			OUT			BALANCE		
		Qty	Cost	Value	Qty	Cost	Value	Qty	Cost	Value
Jul 1	Balance							5	180	900
2	Inv.92843	10	190	1900				5	180	
								10	190	2,800
3	Rec.8743				2	180	360	3	180	

This is a document used by a business to keep the record of stocks. It is used to enter the items in stock and monitor stock inflows and outflows.

Insurance

This is an agreement that involves paying money to an insurance company to assign the responsibility and accountability of costs if there is an accident or injury in one's business. The amount of money charged by the **insurer** (insurance company) to the **insured** to cover for any loss is called the **premium**.

Difference between insurance & assurance

Insurance is the protection against something that might happen in one's business. For example, a motor vehicle insurance for accidents or fire, insurance for one's house. On the other hand, assurance is protection against something that will happen. For example, life assurance because death is a certainty.

Principles of insurance

5. **The pooling of risks** – These are premiums paid by individuals or groups into a pool, managed by an insurance company to compensate for losses.
6. **Utmost good faith** – This states that it is the duty of the insured to disclose all facts to the insurance company. Any fraud or misrepresentation of facts can lead to the cancellation of the contract.
7. **Insurable interest** – This is the situation where the insured must have an interest in the subject matter of the insurance. The interest could be in his or her life, the life of his/her spouse, and the life of any person in whose survival he/she

has a financial interest. For example, the life of the child/children.

8. **Contribution** – If a person has insured identical risks on the same property through different companies, then the amount of the loss is shared between the insurance companies, each one paying a contribution. This prevents the insured from receiving the full compensation from each company and so making a profit.

5. **Proximate cause** – This principle seeks to protect the insurer. They are only liable to replace the insured property if the cause of destruction was the one insured against.

6. **Indemnity** – This refers to a situation when one individual (insurer) takes on the obligation to pay for any loss or damage that has been or might be incurred by another individual (the insured). No one should make a profit for the loss. It restores the insured person to their original position (for example, before the loss occurred).

7. **Subrogation** – According to the principle of subrogation, when the insured is compensated for the losses due to damage to his insured property, then the ownership right of such property shifts to the insurer. For example, if A's car was hit by B's, then A has certain legal rights against B since B was responsible for hitting A's car. However, if A's company took care of the damage, then by the law of subrogation A's insurance company would be entitled to any compensation A received from B.

Types of insurance policies

1. **Life**
   i. **Whole life policies** – In this type of policy, a fixed sum is payable on the death of the insured. The beneficiaries of the insured will be paid.
   ii. **Endowment policies** – Payments are made after some years or on the death of the insured. If death occurs before the end of the endowment period, the beneficiaries of the insured will be paid.

2. **Non-life policies**
   a. **Marine insurance** – This includes:
      i. **Hull insurance** – This covers damage to the ship or any other vessel.
      ii. **Cargo insurance** – Compensation to the owners of cargo (goods) in the event of loss or damage.
      iii. **Ship owner's liability** – This covers loss or damage to third parties, for example, to the crew, passengers, and port facilities.
      iv. **Freight insurance** – This provides the owner of the ship with coverage if the cost of delivering cargo is not paid for by the cargo owner.
   b. **Motor insurance** – Motor vehicle insurance protects a car owner against financial loss due to unpredictable events like auto accidents, fires, and natural disasters. The insurance policy will also respond to pay to third parties for injury or damage to property caused by you in an accident. Motor insurance can be comprehensive or third party.

c. **Business insurance** – This includes:
   i. **Fire** – These covers losses to assets by fire.
   ii. **Burglary** – This covers the losses due to goods stolen and any damage to property caused by theft.
   iii. **Glass insurance** – This covers replacement of windows as well as injury to staff and customers that may be caused by its breakage
d. **Employer's liability and public liability** – These covers accidents to employees through the negligence of the employer and to persons visiting the business as customers.

How insurance lowers risks in a business

1. Insurance helps to compensate for a business after serious incidents such as fire, injury to persons, or theft.
2. This compensation helps the business continue operating after such a financial loss which could have closed the business.

UNIT 5
FACTORS OF PRODUCTION

For a successful operation of the production of goods, some factors must be put into consideration. These factors are simply the resources used by a firm to produce goods and services. There are four major factors of production.

Types of factors of production

1. **Land** – All the natural resources that nature provides to the society. This can be on, above, or below the earth's surface, for example, gold, diamond, oil, rivers, ponds, deserts, and forests.

2. **Labour** – This refers to the human effort involved in production either physical or mental. This includes the skills of the different types of workers (skilled, semi-skilled or unskilled)

3. **Capital** – This refers to all man-made assets that allowed for increased work productivity, such as machinery, buildings, tools, equipment, etc.

4. **Enterprise/entrepreneurial skills** – An entrepreneur identifies a great business opportunity, risks time, and money

to start the business and employs the other factors of production to make an item or offer a service.

Types of capital

1. **Fixed capital** – This refers to the capital, which is invested in purchasing fixed assets for a business. They are long-lasting and do not change. For example, machinery, equipment, etc. Fixed capital cannot be easily turned into cash.
2. **Working capital** – This is the amount of money available for the daily operations of the business. It is calculated by subtracting the current liabilities from current assets. Working capital is used to pay workers, purchase raw materials, etc.
3. **Venture capital** – This is the money provided by investors to start-up businesses.

Role of capital in production

1. It undertakes production that labour would not complete promptly (for example, deep-sea drilling).
2. It improves the quality of items produced by producing goods with fewer defects.
3. It increases productivity with the growth of technology and specialization. It is an important factor as more goods can be produced with the aid of capital.
4. It creates employment opportunities as employees will be hired to produce goods with the help of machines and factories.

Difference between production and productivity

Production is the process of creating or manufacturing goods and services. It also refers to the quantity produced.

Productivity is used to measure the efficiency or rate of production. It is the amount of output (for example, the number of goods produced) per unit of input (for example, labor, equipment, and capital).

Production involves output produced while productivity involves output per unit of input.

Factors influencing productivity

1. Level of education and training.
2. Working conditions.
3. Motivation.
4. Good management.
5. The health of the workforce.

Benefits/importance of productivity

1. Lower cost of producing goods leading to affordability and improvements in the standard of living.
2. Increased productivity enables higher wages for workers.
3. Increased productivity leads to economic growth.

Factors affecting the labour supply

1. The size/categories of a country's labour force.
2. The number of individuals willing and able to work.
3. The opportunity to obtain education and training. This determines both the quality and quantity of labour available in a country.
4. Salary & working conditions of businesses.

Types of production

1. **Primary or extractive production** – This involves extracting raw materials from nature/environment. Examples are quarrying, agriculture, mining, fishing, and forestry.
2. **Secondary production** – This is the 2nd stage of production. It involves taking raw materials and converting them into finished or semi-finished goods. Secondary production refers to either construction or manufacturing industries.
   a. **Manufacturing** – This involves converting raw materials into finished products useful to man.
   b. **Construction** – This is concerned with the construction of buildings, bridges, etc.
3. **Service/tertiary** – These are the provision of services such as transport, communication, tourism, and teaching.

Levels of production

1. **Traditional/subsistence**

This is where people produce goods to meet the basic needs of themselves or their families. It engages in mainly agricultural products, for example, fishing and farming.

2. **Domestic consumption**

This level of production targets the individual, family, community, and even the local market.

3. **Surplus production**

In this level of production, goods are produced in excess to be sold in the local or export markets.

4. **Export production**

This is the production of goods and services only for the purpose of exporting, thereby meeting the needs of a foreign market.

Cottage Industries

A cottage industry is an industry whose labour force consists of family members or individuals working at home with their equipment. Examples are woodwork, pottery, and craft items.

Features of a cottage industry

a) Home-based.
b) Mainly manual.
c) Small scale.
d) Use of local raw material.
e) Use of family members as labour.

Small business

This is a business that employs less than 10 persons and total assets do not exceed $500, 000TT. It is always established on a small scale and in a rural area.

Functions of small business

1. Creates employment for persons living in the area.
2. Provide services that large firms are not willing to produce.
3. Niche markets that allows for new customers to be served.

Advantages of small businesses

1. It creates employment and job opportunities in most rural or economically depressed areas for the generation of income.
2. It automatically increases competition for larger firms.
3. There is no limitation of ideas as new products and business ideas can be introduced, such as event planning.

Disadvantages of small firms
1. The business lacks expertise in certain areas.
2. Owners find it difficult sourcing finance from financial institutions.
3. Limited ability to service customers due to unavailable resources.

Linkage industry

The linkage industry is an industry that is connected or dependent on another industry (the existence of one depends on the other).

Benefits of linkage industries to Caribbean economies
- ✓ Increase in investment.
- ✓ Countries can save on imports.
- ✓ Increased exports through items produced by linkages.
- ✓ Increased standard of living.

Types of linkages

1. **Forward linkage**

This is a type of linkage where the product of one industry becomes the raw material of the other.

Vegetable ─────────────> tourism

2. **Backward linkage**

This is a type of linkage where the demand for one product leads to the establishment of another. For example, a manufacturing firm may link with a firm in the primary phase of production. Other examples: a bakery depends on another business for flour.

Vegetables <───────────── tourism

Craft items <───────────── tourism

Following the above illustration, forward linkages are directed towards consumers while backward linkages are directed towards suppliers.

Effects of growth on a business

1. **Organizational structure**

The organization structure of a business will change as a business grows; More departments to the business structure and more functional managers will report to the owner.

2. **Capital**

More capital will be needed as the business grows. This finance will be needed for:

   a) Additional fixed assets as buildings and machinery.
   b) Increase stock and cash to meet day-to-day expenses.
   c) Hiring more staff.

3. **Use of technology**

Growing businesses are likely to use more technology than a small business. Use of computers
for:

   ➢ Communication internally, for example, the internet.
   ➢ Communication with customers and suppliers through the internet.
   ➢ Conducting secondary market research.

4. **Potential for export**

A growing firm will be able to produce to satisfy both local and export needs since they have the resources (financial, capital & labour, etc.) needed to export products.

How a business grows internally & externally

Areas of internal growth
1. Opening other outlets.
2. Employing more workers.
3. Increasing capital.

Examples of external growth
i. **Joint ventures** – This is a business arrangement where two or more parties agree to pool their resources to accomplish a specific task. This task can be a new project or any other business activity.
ii. **Mergers** – A merger usually involves combining two companies into a single larger company.
iii. **Takeovers/acquisitions** – This is where a company gains control of another company by buying most of its shares.

Natural resources found in Caribbean countries

Country	Natural resources	Industry used
Jamaica	Bauxite, Beaches, Gypsum.	Aluminum, tourism, construction.
Trinidad and Tobago	Gas, oil, asphalt.	Energy production, petroleum, and road construction.
Guyana	Bauxite, gold, oil.	Aluminum, jewelry, petroleum.
Barbados	Gas, limestone.	Energy production and construction.

UNIT 6
MARKETING

MARKET

A market is a place where buyers and sellers trade for a product or service. A market can be physical or virtual with the same goal of bringing the sellers and buyers together, allowing sellers to make some profit while satisfying the buyers with the goods and services they need.

Marketing

Marketing is the process of getting the product or service to the customer for a specific price. This is an important aspect of every business.

Trends in marketing

1. **Social media marketing**

The process of selling a product or service via social media such as Facebook and Instagram.

2. **Integrated marketing**

The process of selling a product or service directly to customers based on their preferences.

Difference between market and marketing

Marketing	Market
A process that identifies what workers need.	A situation where buyers and sellers are brought together.
Products and services are offered to satisfy the worker's needs.	The exchange of goods and services for a specific price.

Marketing mix (4 p's)

The marketing mix is also called the **4 p's** of marketing. It explains the different ways that a product or service is marketed. The marketing mix includes:

1. Product

This includes the products or services produced for customers. It covers how much goods and services to be produced, for whom they should be made, and the type of features to be considered and incorporated.

2. Price

The price is the amount of money that would be charged for the product or service. It is also based on how much customers are willing to pay and whether the firm can make a profit.

3. Place

This is the location that will be used to offer the products or services to the customers.

4. Promotion

The firm must decide what methods would be used to make customers aware of their products. This can be done through sales promotion, advertising, and personal selling.

Marketing activities

These are the steps taken in the marketing of a product or service. The marketing activities are:

1. **Market research**

This is the collection of data and information about a product or service to be offered. It includes information about consumer taste, competitors in the market, and consumer behaviour.

2. **Pricing**

The firm must decide on a suitable price that consumers are willing to pay for the product or service to be offered. Therefore, allowing them to make a profit through the sale of goods and services.

3. **Packaging**

This is the processing of safely labeling the product to attract customers to purchase the product.

4. **Branding**

This is the use of names, colours, or signs to make the product different from competitors. Consumers would in turn become aware of the firm's product.

5. **Sales promotion**

Strategies that encourage consumers to buy more in a short period. For example, a buy-one-get-one-free promotion.

6. **Advertising**

This is the activity of using different forms of communication to persuade consumers to buy a product or service. For example, advertising on Television, or through the social media.

7. **Distribution**

This is the process of getting the product or service close to the potential customers.

Factors influencing consumer behaviour

Consumer behaviour – activities considered when purchasing and using a product. They are as follows:

1. **Income**

The income of consumers will determine what they can or cannot afford.

2. **Brand loyalty**

A firm will try to persuade customers to purchase their product over another competitor. This is building brand loyalty by having repeated purchases by the consumer.

3. **Tradition**

The culture and customs of consumers will influence what products they purchase. For example, purchasing Kellogg's cornflakes and Kerigold milk.

4. **Taste**

Consumers will purchase products based on what they prefer. A business must be aware of the consumers' taste to offer the products preferred.

5. **Price**

Depending on the features of a product the price charged will be different. Where the product has the same features, the cheaper product will be purchased by consumers.

6. **Price of substitutes**

Where consumers have a variety of products to choose from, they will choose the product that meets their needs at the most affordable price.

Factors affecting packaging and presentation of goods

Packaging

Packaging is the outer wrapper or container of an item. Marketers package and label their products to attract and encourage potential buyers to purchase the product.

Factors that influence packaging are:

1. Provision for easy handling and transportation from one place to another.
2. It must be able to be differentiated from competitors.
3. It must allow the company name and logo to be identified by customers as a brand.
4. Customers must be informed on the packaging information about the product content, features, expiry date, and nutritional value.
5. It must protect the product and ensure that customers get an undamaged product.

Methods of promoting sales are:

1. **Personal selling** – This includes the selling of a product or service directly to customers by moving from one place to another. For example, selling insurance by an agent.
2. **Public relations** – Presenting a positive image of the business to customers, community, and the government. For example, presenting awards and sponsoring community

activities.
3. **Sales promotion** – This strategy encourages consumers to buy more in a short period, for example, buy-one-get-one-free promotion.
4. **Advertising** – The use of different forms of communication to encourage and attract consumers to purchase a product.

Types of advertising

1. **Informative advertising** – Presenting facts about a product to potential customers. Information about the product benefits are given in this type of advertising.
2. **Persuasive advertising** – Presenting information to customers that entices them to purchase a product based on emotions.
3. **Comparative advertising** – Comparing the features of two products at the same time. The benefits of one product will be highlighted more than others.
4. **Reminder advertising** – Reminds consumers that the product is currently available for purchase on the market. This is used for products where there are many competitors.
5. **Loss leader** – The pricing of one product very cheaply to attract customers into the store. Once in the store, the customer would then purchase other items.
6. **Social media** – The process of selling a product or service via the internet using websites such as Facebook, Twitter, and Instagram.
7. **Coupons** – These are clips that can be taken off a product or used as a discount to encourage customers to buy the

product.

Functions of advertising

1) To introduce new products to the market.
2) To assist with creating competition.
3) To help with increasing sales.
4) To remind customers that the product still exists.

Techniques in selling

1) Providing discounts to customers.
2) Online shopping.
3) Offering good after-sale service
4) Giving free samples.
5) Clearly display of products.

Why consumer organizations exist

Consumer organizations exist to protect the rights of consumers. They seek information about the goods and services that consumers purchase so that informed decisions can be made.

Types of consumer organizations

1. Consumer Affairs Division

This is an agency that provides advice and assistance to citizens. They offer information about products and services that are advertised.

2. The Ombudsman

A person appointed by the government to investigate malpractices or injustice suffered by individuals when dealing with government offices.

Functions of Ombudsman

a) Investigates complaints made by individuals.

b) Make recommendations to correct the wrongdoing of state agencies.

3. Bureau of standards

This is a government agency that protects consumers by ensuring that goods are produced using quality raw materials and under safe conditions.

Terms of sale

1) Hire purchase

This is a short-term credit that is given when an item is purchased. The customer makes an initial payment, followed by monthly payments over some time until it is paid off.

Advantages of hire purchase

a) The customer has the immediate use of a product.
b) The customer will become the owner of the product after it is paid off.

Disadvantages of hire purchase

a) A very expensive form of purchasing goods.
b) Goods are not the property of the buyer until the last instalment is made.

2) Cash sales

This is created when a customer pays money for the exchange of a product or service.

Advantages of cash sales

a) There is no risk that the customer will lose the product as under hire purchase.

3) Layaway

The buyer makes an agreement to pay for the goods on instalment. The goods remain with the seller until all payments are made

4) **Trade discount**

This is a discount given to buyers when products are purchased from a supplier.

5) **Cash discount**

A cash discount is an amount given to the buyer for prompt payment.

Advantages of cash discounts

a) It encourages prompt payment.
b) It causes a faster movement of stock.

The Role of Customer Service

Customer services is the assistance given by a company to its customers when products or services are used.

Offering good customer services benefits the consumer by:

1. Ensures customers receive the type of product or service they require.
2. It ensures that there is effective communication between the business and the consumer on how the product should and should not be used.
3. The adherence of copyrights laws is ensured. That is, the company is the only place that can offer information to consumers. For example, the authorized dealers.
4. It is an effective way to distribute goods, services, and information to consumers.

Forms of customer service

1) Warranty
This is a written guarantee issued to the purchaser of an article by its manufacturer. It promises to repair or replace it if necessary, within a specified period.

2) After-sale service
This is all the help and information that the buyer provides to customers **after** they have bought a product or service.

3) Feedback
Information about reactions to a product or service, which is used as a basis for improvement.

4) Online chat
To participate with one or more people, through the **Internet**, in a real-time conversation about the company products or service offered.

5) Toll-free numbers/call centres
A **toll-free** telephone **number** a telephone **number** that is billed for all arriving calls instead of the customer being charged.

6) Suggestion box
A **suggestion box** is a device for obtaining additional comments, questions, and requests from customers.

7) Surveys
This is the document given to customers with questions about the product or service offered to them. The information is used to make improvements by the business

Intellectual property rights

This is a right held by a person or company to be the sole user for a specific idea or plan without competition from competitors for a specific period.

Types of intellectual property rights

1. **Patent**

This is an official document granting a right. For example, a franchisee is given a patent to reproduce the product such as KFC chicken.

2. **Trademark**

This is a distinguishing mark attached to goods that have been registered and cannot be used by another company.

3. **Copyright**

This right protects creators and innovators with their original work. This includes music, painting, movie, and writing. Persons must request permission to use these works from the creators of these works. Copyright allows creators to be paid for their work.

4. **Industrial design**

This is the way a manufactured product is designed by a company. Intellectual property rights can offer protection to a manufacturer with their unique way of designing their products. For example, coke contour bottle.

UNIT 7
LOGISTICS AND SUPPLY CHAIN

Logistics

This is ensuring that material and workers are in the right place at the right time for a business to achieve its objectives.

Supply chain operations

These are the systems, processes, resources involved in moving a product or service from supplier to customer.

Components of logistics

The components of logistics are the forward and reverse flow of goods

1. **Traditional or forward flow of goods** – Traditional flow of goods is the movement of products from the factory to the consumer. It includes product development, manufacturing & distribution of products.

2. **Reverse flow of goods** – This refers to the processes associated with managing products beyond manufacturing and the final sale. It includes repair, returns, repackaging for resale, proper disposal, etc.

3. **Storage of goods** – This is deciding where goods would be

stored until sold by the supplier to the customers.
4. **Insurance** – This is a service to provide coverage for products if lost or damaged during distribution.

Activities in supply chain operations

1. **Transformation of natural resources** – This involves changing raw materials into a product that can be used by customers.
2. **Movement and storage of raw materials** – This ensures that raw materials for production are transported by a suitable means and that they are stored in a safe place.
3. **Processing raw materials into finished goods** – This involves changing raw materials into finished goods using a manufactured process.
4. **Storage of work-in-progress & finished goods** – This involves the storage of partly finished and finished goods until ready to be distributed to customers.
5. **Delivering the finished product** from point of origin (Supplier) to the point of destination (Customer) – This is ensuring that the product or service reaches the intended customer.

Distribution chain

This is how a product moves from the manufacturer to the consumer. This includes:

Producer/manufacturer

This is someone or a business that creates and supplies goods or services. Producers combine raw materials, labour, and capital to create a product or service.

Wholesaler

This is a business or a person that buys goods from a manufacturer in large quantities and then sells in small quantities to retailers such as shops.

Retailer

A person, shop, or business that buys from a manufacturer or supplier and sells directly to consumers in small quantities.

Consumer

A person who buys goods for personal use and not for resale.

Difference between multi-modal and intermodal transport

Intermodal shipping

This is when the business cargo (goods) is handled by **different shipping companies** using several modes of transport. This would require a different contract with all shipping companies for each part of the journey.

Multimodal shipping

This is where **one company** handles all parts of the journey. For example, one company is responsible for moving your shipment for the entire journey using different means of transport.

Modes of transport

Transport involves the movement of products or people from one place to another. Goods can be transported by the following ways:

Air transportation

This is the movement of goods using airlines.

Advantages of air transportation
   a. Fastest mode of transport for perishables, medical supplies, and important documents.

b. Shorter travel times for goods to arrive for distribution.
   c. It is a reliable form of transport.

Disadvantages of air transportation
   a. Expensive due to the high cost of operating an aircraft.
   b. Cannot be used for heavy or bulky items.
   c. Other forms of transport are needed to and from the airport.

Rail transportation

This is used to transport heavy or bulky goods using rail tracks. Not commonly used in the Caribbean.

Advantages of rail transportation
   a. Faster than road transport.
   b. Can carry heavy or bulky goods that are impossible or expensive by air or road.
   c. Fewer workers are needed with rail transport.

Disadvantages of rail transportation
   a. Railway stations or lines are located only in certain areas
   b. Goods need to be transported to and from the train.

Road transportation

This involves the use of vans and trucks to deliver goods to customers, transporting goods by road.

Advantages of road transportation
   a. Offers door to door service.
   b. Able to reach customers who cannot be reached in other ways.

Disadvantages of road transportation
   a. Congested towns and cities can slow down delivery.
   b. Some roads may be in extremely poor conditions.

Marine transportation

This is the shipment of goods by sea and other waterways. It involves using containers, oil tankers, etc.

Advantages of marine transportation

a. It is cheaper than road, air, or rail transport.
b. Access to all countries.

Disadvantages of marine transportation

a. Slow method of transport and not suitable for rapid delivery.
b. Shipping schedules may not be frequent.

Pipeline transportation

This is the transportation of goods or material (liquid or gases) through a pipe. For example, crude and refined petroleum and fuels, such as oil and natural gas.

Advantages of pipeline transportation

a. It involves exceptionally low energy consumption.
b. It needs little maintenance.
c. Pipelines are safe, accident-free, and environmentally friendly.

Disadvantages of pipeline transportation

a. It is not flexible. For example, it can be used only for a few fixed points.
b. It is difficult to make security arrangements for pipelines.
c. Underground pipelines cannot be easily repaired, and detection of leakage is also difficult.

Digital delivery

This involves downloading information directly from the internet to a home computer. For example, an anti-virus software, document, audio, or video.

Advantages of digital delivery
   a. It provides the customer with their desired product instantly.
   b. The cost is relatively cheap.

Disadvantages of digital delivery
   a. It requires high-speed internet to be effective.
   b. It can lose data or information if it was not stored properly.

The role (importance) of transport in marketing
1. Ensures the **fast-tracking of commodities** – This involves knowing the possible time it would take the goods to arrive for distribution to customers.
2. Ensures **security of supply** – This means that by having a reliable transportation system ensures that goods are always available to customers on time.
3. **Cost reduction** – The best transportation method should be chosen for the sale of a product. This ensures that costs are kept at a minimum.

Importance of transport in trade
1. Increases employment – More workers are needed to ensure that goods are transported on time both locally and regionally.
2. It makes available a wider variety of goods to consumers – Consumers now have a variety of goods to choose from, because of better transportation methods worldwide.

3. It brings goods from producer to consumer anywhere in the world which increases foreign trade.

Transport documents
Bill of lading

This is used when goods are imported by sea. The shipper (exporter) sends it to the importer. It contains information as:

1. Shipper/exporter.
2. Consignee/importer.
3. Name of vessel and port of destination.
4. Details and weight of cargo.
5. Freight costs involved.

Import licenses

This is an official document from a government that allows the import of certain goods or services into a country. For example, Toyota cars.

Airway bill

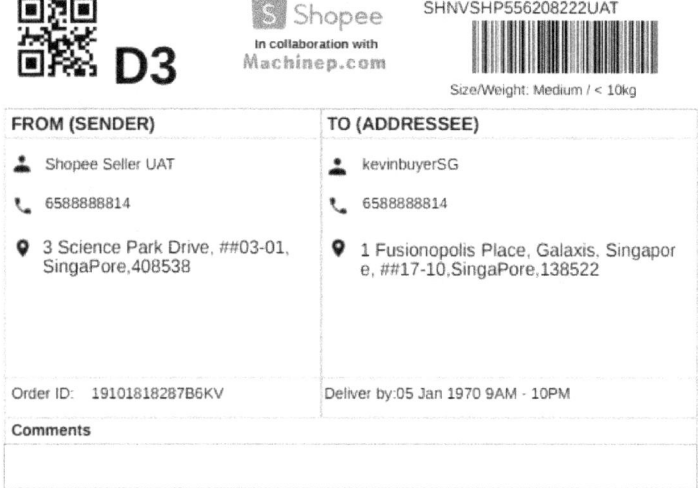

This is a document used for air transport of goods. It serves as a receipt of goods by an airline (the carrier), as well as a contract of carriage between the shipper and the carrier.

Information on airway bill

1. Shipper's name, address, tel. number and signature.
2. Receiver/consignee's telephone number and contact details.
3. Total weight.
4. Payment details.
5. Number of packages and descriptions.
6. Time and date package were picked up by or delivered to the courier.

Advantages and Challenges (disadvantages) of Supply Chain Operations

Advantages of supply chain operations

1. It provides a better quality of life to customers as more goods and services are made available.
2. It leads to wealth creation as new businesses are created within the chain.
3. It provides new and innovative job opportunities including entrepreneurship, for example, telemarketing.

Disadvantages of supply chain operations

1. Political instability can affect operations.
2. Poor Management.
3. Products can be obsolete easily.
4. Natural disasters can hinder the delivery and ordering of goods.

Problems encountered in distribution

a) Relationship between the availability of airport, harbour and docking facilities and the efficient distribution of goods.
b) Delayed shipment, spoilage, misdirection of goods, inadequate warehousing facilities, lack of proper security measures, industrial unrest, and ineffective communication.

Measures to solve problems in distribution

1. Avoid holding large stocks.
2. Select the appropriate channel of distribution based on the product.
3. Careful labelling and documentation.
4. Ensure goods are insured.

5. Government intervention.
6. Use of security cameras.

Impact of information technology on logistic and supply chain operations

Forms of technology

1. **Global positioning system (GPS)**

This is a system of satellites and computers that can determine the location of an object. It helps the business to know where its products are in the distribution process, as well as the tracking of items delivered.

2. **Portnet**

This helps the port and shipping communities to increase productivity and save costs through the greater use of information technology by the movement and tracking of cargo both on land and sea. Portnet simplifies millions of processes for customers locally and globally.

3. **Geographic information system (GPS)**

This is a graphic information system that is used by a business to create solutions and strategies. This information assists a business in the analysis of data to run more efficiently. The company can instantly receive requests and see a map of all retailers in the area.

4. **Telemarketing**

This means contacting customers and potential customers by telephone or using a fax or internet.

5. **E-commerce**

This is the buying and selling of goods using the internet. This allows for fast and efficient distribution of goods globally.

6. **Global logistics providers**

These include companies that distribute goods to customers. For example, FedEx, DHL, and Amazon Logistics.

7. **Logistic hub**

This is a specific area that deals with activities related to transportation, organization, separation, coordination, and distribution of goods nationally and internationally. For example, Singapore is the world's number 1 logistic hub and the proposed Jamaica logistic hub. Once completed, the Jamaica logistic hub will be the 4th major logistic hub in the world.

How Logistic Contributes to the Competitiveness of Business

When a company creates an efficient logistic and supply chain distribution system, it contributes to its efficiency by:

1. **Competitive advantage**

This is where one business is more efficient at a process rather than its competitors. For example, one business can receive and distribute their products in less time than their competitors, then customers would prefer to buy from that business.

2. **Logistics improves competitiveness**

This is ensuring that all material and personnel needed are in the right place at the right time which increases the business competitiveness over other businesses.

3. **Comparative cost advantage**

This is where a business can produce goods and services at a lower cost than its competitors.

Party logistics
Global logistic providers
1PLs are businesses that invest in their own means of transportation, support tools, and available resources such as human resources to organize and carry out logistics activities to meet their needs. A 1PL can be companies considered as self-logistics like manufacturer, trader, importer/exporter, wholesaler, retailer, or distributor in the international commerce field. It can also be an institution such as a government department or an individual or family moving from one place to another.

2PL aims to provide single services, contributing to a small aspect of the customer's supply chain. Usually, 2PLs are sea, land, or air carriers. Some examples of 2PL are freight forwarders, freight brokers, customs brokers, export management companies, exporting trading companies, shipping associations, shipper's agents, and export packing companies.

In general, **3PL** and **4PL** activities are involved in the supply chain activities from input materials to output products, transporting to the recipient. Some examples of 3PLs are DHL and FedEx. They are the leading companies in providing global logistics services, including services from shipping by air to air, planning, and optimization of transportation networks, agent management, security system management, incoterm, and cargo insurance. While, for example, some companies are currently providing 4PL services such as UPS, XPO Logistics, and Geodis Wilson company.

However, the most outstanding example of **5PL** focuses on E-logistics, Logistics based on e-commerce. The characteristics of 5PL are the systems, Order Management System (OMS), Warehouse Management System (WMS), and Transport Management System (TMS). These three systems are closely related together in a unified system and information technology.

UNIT 8
BUSINESS FINANCE

In any business, finance plays a key role in its operations. The business activity needs money to run, operate, and to expand the business in the future.

Financial institutions

Commercial banks

These are financial institutions that accept deposits, offer loans to individuals, companies, businesses, and the general public with the aim of making a profit through interest. Also, they offer other services such as payment of salaries. Some examples of these institutions are RBC, RBL, Scotiabank, and First Citizens Bank.

Functions of commercial banks

1. **Acceptance of deposits** (money) from customers – Commercial Banks accept deposits from individuals and firms for safekeeping and then allow payments to be made from these deposits.

2. **Provision of loans** to individuals and firms – Finance is made available to customers for the start of business or personal events. These loans are then refunded within a certain timeframe.
3. **Provision of a smart transaction system** – Payment processing is made and received by customers through internet banking and automatic transfers.
4. They allow the **issuing of bank drafts and bank cheques** to customers.
5. They offer **investment services** and safekeeping of documents via safe deposit boxes.

Central banks

A Central bank is a monetary authority set up by a government to issue notes and coin, control the money supply, and regulate the banking system in the country.

Functions of the central banks

1. **They issue notes and coins** – The central bank controls all the activities and issues of a country's currency. This is to prevent the individual and the public from losing confidence in the money supply of the country.
2. **They act as the bankers for the commercial banks** – All commercial banks have deposits in the central bank. This gives the central bank some control over the commercial bank activities. For example, the central bank allows the other banks to pay each other (RBC paying Scotiabank) using these deposits at the central bank.

3. **They act as the government's bankers** – They allow the government to receive, make payments, and borrow when needed.
4. **They are the lender of last resort** – If the commercial banks have a shortage of money then the central bank can lend some money to the banks to prevent them from folding or falling. However, the interest rate charged is exceedingly high.
5. **They regulate the banking system** to ensure that banks do not give out too many loans at one time.

Role of central banks over commercial banks

The central bank is responsible for ensuring that commercial banks do not engage in dangerous activities such as lending to persons that are not able to pay back their loans. If banks are not supervised by the central bank, then customers can lose their money if the bank fails.

Examples:
   a. **In Trinidad and Tobago** – the Financial Supervision Department of the Central Bank supervises all other banks.
   b. **In Jamaica** – The central bank supervises all other banks.

1. **Credit unions**

This is a financial institution (non-bank) that brings members' savings together, to provide members with low-cost loans when needed. For example, the Eastern Credit Union and Police Credit Union.

2. **Agricultural development bank**

In Trinidad and Tobago, this is a bank owned by the government that provides farmers with low-interest loans to purchase agricultural machinery, equipment, and land for the expansion of the agriculture industry. Farmers can also save with the bank as well. For example, ADB – Agricultural Development Banks.

3. Insurance companies

These are financial institutions that provide life and non-life (investment, vehicle, etc.) services to customers. Loans can also be gained from the cash value in life insurance policies.

4. Building societies

A financial organization that pays interest on investments by its members and lends capital for the purchase or improvement of houses. For example, TBLA – Trinidad Building and Loan Association.

Services offered by financial institutions

1. **Loans including overdrafts** – Financial institutions make their profit by offering loans to customers. This can be for the purchase of a home, car, or start of a business. Overdraft is where customers are given access to more money than they have in their accounts. Interest is paid for the amount given.

2. **Savings and deposits** – Financial institutions allow customers to deposit and earn interest on their savings. This can be used to build wealth over time.

3. **Making payments** – Financial institutions provide customers with 'plastic money' in the form of cards that can be used to buy goods and services from businesses. For example, debit cards and credit cards.

4. **Investments** – Financial institutions offer customers advice on issues such as pension plans, stock exchange investments, and other long-term financial plans.
5. **Night safe deposit** – This is a service offered by commercial banks where customers can deposit cash outside business hours.
6. **Online banking** – This is a service offered to customers where they can access their accounts via the internet to make transfers or pay bills online. Therefore, reducing the time to go to a bank.
7. **Deposit boxes** – This is a service where customers can deposit cash or cheques using an envelope into a box, which will then be cleared by the bank. It is fast and prevents customers from having to join the queue at the bank.
8. **ATM/ABM services** – This is a service where customers can withdraw, deposit, and transfer funds using a machine without having to see a teller.

Regulatory Bodies

These are government authorities that are responsible for monitoring different businesses to protect customers.

1. **Central bank**

This is a monetary authority set up by a national government to issue notes and coin, control the money supply, and regulate the banking system in the country.

2. **Jamaica Deposit Insurance Company (JDIC)**

This is a government authority created to protect customers' deposits and promote financial stability in the country.

3. Financial Services Commission (FSC)

FSC is a government authority responsible for the inspection and supervision of a country's financial institutions.

Roles/Functions of regulatory bodies

1. To monitor, control, and guide various industry sectors to protect consumers.
2. To enforce regulations and licenses of various financial activities, including depository, lending, collection, and money transmission activities.

Ways the central banks/JDIC/FSC influence financial institutions

1. They can adjust the **interest rates** charges by financial institutions at any time. For example, if they increase the interest rate for the banks then it would be awfully expensive to take a loan. Therefore, customers will not want to take loans (vis-versa).
2. They can **increase or decrease** the required amount that must be kept as a deposit. This will affect how much money is available for customers to borrow.

How individuals manage personal income

1. **Budget** – Individuals can use a budget to decide how their money earned will be spent. It creates a guide as to what is important for the person.
2. **Savings** – Part of a personal income should be set aside as a form of saving. This can be used to cover any emergencies that may occur from time to time.
3. **Investments** – This involves putting money where interest

can be earned in the future. Over time the money would grow.
4. **Financial advising** – Seeking the assistance of a person knowledgeable about investing one's income for growth can be used. This will aid overtime in increasing a person's wealth.

Difference between savings and investments

Savings and Investments are technically related, but they distinct from each other. The definition of terms below indicates the difference between savings and investments.

Savings

This refers to income that is put aside rather than spending, the money is reserved. Simply put, any income that is not spent is referred to as savings. This amount of money is usually the leftover when the cost of an individual's consumer expenditure is subtracted from the total disposable income accumulated over time. So, Savings does not entail the absence of spending.

Forms of saving

1. **Sou sou** – This is where a group of people bring an equal amount of money for some time. For example, 1 month, 3 months, or 6 months.
2. **Credit unions** – These are non-commercial banks that are owned and controlled by members. They promote saving and offer loans at a reasonable interest rate.
3. **Banks** – They offer a range of saving and fixed deposit accounts. Saving accounts include regular accounts where money is saved at a low-interest rate. While a fixed deposit

account is one where higher interest rates are paid for saving money over some time. For example, 1 year.

Investment

Investments can be defined in two ways:
1. By a **company spending money** on expanding a business or buying new equipment to make a profit in the future.
2. This is the investment by an individual **putting aside their saving** into financial instruments which would bring a future return.

Forms of investments

1. **Stock market** - This is where the money is invested in company shares by individuals on the stock market.
2. **Unit trust/mutual funds** - These are companies that attract individuals to buy shares in different companies. Each individual is given UNITS depending on the amount invested.
3. **Government bonds** – These are instruments offered by the government for individuals to invest a certain sum of money for a fixed period. For example, 1 year. Interest is then paid on the amount invested.
4. **Money invested into a new or existing business** – This allows for profits to be gained from the business activities, thereby gaining future wealth.
5. **Buying property as an investment** – When the value of the property increases, the wealth of the individual also increases. Additionally, rental income can also be earned from the property.

Short-term financing

This is the money needed for the running of the day-to-day operation of a business. Usually, in less than one year.

Types of short-term financing
1. **Trade credit** – It is a credit extended by the supplier to the business to pay for goods later. For example, 3 months.
2. **Commercial bank loans** – This is money loaned by a bank for the day-to-day running if a business.
3. **Instalment credits** – The process of paying off a loan in a fixed number of payments. For example, 10 months.
4. **Private money lenders** – These are private individuals that give loans to businesses for their daily operations.
5. **Advances from customers** – This is where customers pay for goods before receiving them. This early payment is then used to tun the business operation.
6. **Venture capitalists** – These are wealthy individuals that provide loans to businesses for a share in their future profits.
7. **Crowdfunding** – The process of funding a business by getting a small amount of money from many people via the internet.
8. **Angel investor** – These are wealthy individuals who give money to businesses in exchange for a share in the ownership of the business.

Long-term financing

This is money needed for the running of a business operation over one year and beyond.

Types of long-term financing

1. **Loans from the government** - The government can provide low-interest loans to businesses for the running of the day-to-day operations. This can help the business plan for its future growth.
2. **Debentures** – These are loans given by one business to another business for the financing of the growth of the business. Interest is paid on these loans.
3. **Shares** – This is where a company sells shares to raise money to finance its long-term plans for the business. Shareholders are then paid dividends for their investment into the company.
4. **Mortgages** – This is where banks or credit unions provide loans to purchase property or to expand the business. Interest is then paid on the amount borrowed.

Personal sources of capital for starting a business

1. Family and friends
2. Personal savings
3. Government grants
4. Loans
5. Shares (equity)
6. Venture capital
7. Crowdfunding

Financial records

Financial recording is the process of recording financial data in a business. These are two ways to record information:

1. **Single entry records** – This is where information is recorded once in the accounting books of the business. For example, in

a receipt book.

2. **Double-entry record** – This is where financial information is recorded in at least two places in the accounting books. There must be a debit or credit entry.

Financial statements

Financial statements are documents prepared to show how the business is performing. For example, if a profit or loss is being made.

Types of financial statements

1. Income statement (trading and profit and loss account)

This is a statement that shows what profit or loss was made by the business for a particular year.

2. Balance sheet

This is a financial statement that shows the assets, liabilities, and capital of the business. Assets are things owned (cash, equipment, and motor van), liabilities are things owed (loans, debentures, and creditors). Capital is the money invested into the business. This document is usually completed once a year.

3. Cash flow statement

This is a statement that shows how much money flows into the business (income) and how much money flows out the business (expenses) for a month.

UNIT 9
RESPONSIBILITIES (ROLES) OF GOVERNMENT IN AN ECONOMY

The government plays an important role in the economy of every state. These are responsibilities of the government concerning the economy of a country.

Responsibilities of a government

1. **Security of the state** – A government is responsible for protecting its citizens and institutions against crime, military attacks, and terrorism activities. For example, the Ministry of National Security.
2. **Protection and general welfare of citizens** – This is where the government seeks to ensure the health, peace, and safety of its citizens by providing social services. For example, the Ministry of Health.
3. **Job security and severance benefits to workers** – This is

the protection of workers jobs and ensuring that workers are compensated if there is job loss.
4. **Protection of the environment** – This is the practice of protecting the natural environment for the benefit of both the environment and humans. For example, the Environment Management Authority (EMA).
5. **Maintenance of a safe environment for investors** – A government should enjoy that the country has political stability. This ensures that investors have confidence in the country's economy.
6. **Regulation of business activity** – This involves providing clear guidelines for setting up and running a business legally. For example, the legal documents required and taxes to be paid.

Ways a government can influence businesses to protect the environment

This is done by creating policies or legislation on:

a) **Green technology** – This is the use of technology that is environmentally friendly that conserves natural resources. The purpose of this technology is to reduce global warming.

b) **Reforestation** – This refers to the replanting of trees on land that has previously had trees but were previously cut down.

c) **Proper disposal of waste** – This is done by having regular garbage collection in residential areas.

d) **Zoning laws** – These are laws that guide where homes and companies can be built.

Taxation

Taxation refers to an obligatory financial charge or levy imposed by the government organization upon a legal entity (taxpayer). The primary aim of tax is to fund government spending and various public expenditures in a country. It is an involuntary financial charge.

Reasons why the government charges for taxes:

a) To curb inflation by reducing the supply of money in the economy.

b) To remove competition from local goods to protect the infant (new) industries by taxing imports at high rates.

c) To encourage persons to buy local produce to increase growth for local businesses.

d) To achieve greater **equality in the distribution of wealth** and income by taxing the higher income earners to provide social services for most citizens.

Difference between direct and indirect taxes

1. **Direct taxes** – These are taxes paid directly to the government by the taxpayer. It is paid by individuals and organizations.

Examples of direct taxes are:

i. **Income tax** – Charged on an individual's income/salary.
ii. **Corporation tax** – Taxes charged on the profits of a company.
iii. **Capital gains tax** – A tax charged on profit from the sale of property or an investment.
iv. **Capital transfer tax** – This is a tax on the passing

of property from one person (or entity) to another, for example, by a gift or inheritance.

2. **Indirect taxes** – This is a tax charged on goods and services and is usually paid by manufacturers or importers.

Examples of indirect taxes:

i. **Custom duty** – This is a tax charged on imports and exports of goods.

ii. **Excise duty** – A tax on the sale of a good or service such as fuel, tobacco, and alcohol.

iii. **Purchase tax** – A tax added to the price of goods sold to consumers; the purchaser rather than the seller pays this tax. For example, a car tax.

iv. **Stamp duty** – A tax collected for the placing of a stamp on certain legal documents, for example, placing of stamp for the purchase of a house

v. **Consumption tax** – This is a tax on the purchase of a good or service. People are taxed based on how much they consume.

Types of consumption taxes

a. **GCT** (General Consumption Tax) – This is a tax added to the final price paid by the consumer for goods and services imported or bought locally.

b. **SCT** (Special Consumption Tax) – It is charged on alcoholic beverages, tobacco, petroleum products, and motor vehicles.

c. **VAT** (Value added tax) – A tax charged on products at every point where value is being added, starting from production to final retail purchase. The consumer pays the VAT. For example, if a product costs $100 and there is a 15% VAT, the consumer pays $115 to the merchant. The merchant keeps $100 and remits $15 to the government.

Forms of assistance offered by the government to businesses

a. **Lending capital and technical assistance** – The government can provide loans for the start of a new business. Technical assistance can also be given to start the business. For example, the National Entrepreneurship Development Company, NEDCO, and ADB

b. **Training and human resource development** – The government can set up training sessions to help guide persons who want to start their own business. For example, (NEDCO) and the UWI.

c. **Research and information centres** – The government can provide centres for information that are relevant to businesses through research centres. For example, CARDI (Caribbean Agricultural Research and Development Institute)

d. **Providing subsidies and grants** – The government may also encourage the start or expansion of businesses by giving subsidies and grants which will not be repaid.

Social services provided by government

a. **Healthcare** – Governments provide access to hospitals, clinics, and specialist doctors to citizens.

b. **National insurance** – A compulsory payment made by employees and employers for the government to pay persons who are sick, unemployed, or retired.

c. **Education** – The government can ensure that a country's

citizens have access to schools from kindergarten to university level. This helps to develop the human resource of the country.
d. **Roads and transportation** – The government of a country should ensure that there are proper roads and a good transportation system. This will create greater opportunities for businesses to open and employment created.

UNIT 10

TECHNOLOGY AND GLOBAL BUSINESS ENVIRONMENT

National Income

This is the total output of a country over a year. It is measured in money value by the total production of goods and services.

Importance of national income

The government must estimate the state of the economy and the flow of wealth in the country. For example, goods and services produced, distributed, and consumed by the economy.

Measures of national income

1. **Gross Domestic Product (GDP)** – This is the total value of all the output produced within a country over a year. The word **'domestic'** refers to income earned from local production **only**.

2. **Gross National Product (GNP)** – This is the total money

value of all output produced over one year both within a country and from overseas investment. **GNP = GDP plus Overseas investments.**
3. **Net National Product (NNP)** – This is the total value of goods produced and services provided in a country for one year less depreciation of capital goods (for example, Machines). **NNP = GNP – depreciation**

Difficulties in the calculation of national income

1. Access to information on goods and services produced may have to be estimated.
2. The hidden economy has income that is not included. For example, drug trafficking.
3. Some figures may be double counted which distorts the figures.

How GDP, GNP, and NNP affect economic growth, economic development, standard to living and quality of life

These measures are used to assess how well a country is doing in the following ways:

1. **Economic growth** – This is the increase in productive capacity. It entails the ability to produce more goods and services of a country's economy. It provides a means for achieving a higher **standard of living** for citizens.
2. **Economic development** – The process of improving the **quality of life** of a country's citizens. Economic development is:
   a. The reduction of unemployment.
   b. The reduction of underemployment.

c. The reduction of poverty.
d. The reduction in the inequalities in the distribution of wealth.

The role of education in economic growth and development

Human resource is the total physical and mental abilities of persons in a country. Investment in education is needed for the economic growth and development. Education increases the productivity of individuals who are trained to be more efficient.

International trade

This is the buying and selling of goods and services between countries.

Reasons for international trade

1. Natural resources – Some countries may rely on another for the provision of natural resources such as land, labour, capital, or enterprise to produce the goods that they need.
2. Sufficient Production – A country may be unable to produce the sufficient goods and services they need in the quantities or of the quality that they require.
3. Climate condition – Some countries may dim it fit to depend on others to trade for certain foods they are unable to produce due to some climatic issues. For example, wheat in the United States.
4. Foreign investment – International trade allows for foreign direct investment (FDI), which allows individuals in one country to invest money in foreign companies and other assets.

Benefits of international trade

1. Provides employment.
2. Prevents the development of monopolies in a country.
3. Output is increased because of specialization.
4. allows access to a wide variety of goods.

Economic institutions in the region and globally

The major economic institutions and systems are:

1. **Caribbean Community (CARICOM)** – The Caribbean Community and Common Market (CARICOM) was formed to solve some of the region's development problems.

Functions of CARICOM

a. To improve the standard of living in its member countries.
b. To encourage economic development.
c. To promote full employment of labour as well as the efficient use of other factors of production.
d. To increase trade with other developing economies.
e. To increase the international competitiveness of member countries.

2. **Caribbean Single Market and Economy (CSME)** – The Caribbean Single Market and Economy is a proposed integration agreement involving no barriers between Caribbean countries, so that goods and services, people, capital, and technology can move freely within the Caribbean.

Function of CSME

a. Trade is created with new trading countries.

b. There is free trade with no tariffs between countries.
c. There are free movement of capital, goods, services, and people.
d. A large market with increased sales.
e. The attraction of foreign direct investments (FDI).

3. **Caribbean Development Bank (CDB)** – The CDB was formed in 1970 with the aim of promoting economic co-operation and integration as well as economic growth and development among Caribbean economies.

Functions of CDB

a. To promote private and public investment.
b. To expand international trade within CARICOM countries.
c. To provide capital for developmental projects.
d. To help other financial institutions in the CARICOM countries.

4. **World Bank also called International Bank for Reconstruction and Development (IBRD)** - They aim to assist and encourage long-term international investment by directly lending money in projects that are good commercial risks but where capital is not available.

Functions of the World Bank and IBRD

a. Provides capital for developmental projects in member countries.
b. Assists with developmental projects in member countries by giving advice and technical support.

5. **Organization of American States (OAS)** – The main purpose is to provide collective security, regional co-

operation, and the peaceful settlement of disputes among its member countries.

Functions of OAS

a. To promote the peaceful settlement of disputes among members.
b. To provide a combined security force for all members.
c. To encourage co-operation in trade, social, and cultural activities.

6. **World Trade Organization (WTO)** – This is an international organization that provides guidance on how international trade should take place among its members.

Functions of WTO

a. It provides a code of conduct on how international trade should be conducted.
b. It provides a forum for the settlement of any disputes among members.
c. Topics of concern can be negotiated among its members.

7. **International Monetary Fund (IMF)** – This is an international organization that fosters financial stability, international trade, promote high employment, sustainable economic growth, and reduces poverty.

Functions of the IMF

a. It keeps track of the economic development in member countries.
b. It monitors the financial and economic policies of member countries.

Major Economic Problems in the Caribbean and Solutions

	Problems	Solutions
1.	Unemployment	The provision of education and skill acquisition training with great job opportunities.
2.	Capital Shortage	Encouraging foreign investors to establish investments in the local economy.
3.	Economic dualism	Providing development in all areas of the economy.
4.	Brain drain	Offering attractive payments to highly qualified persons.
5.	Overpopulation	Introducing a countrywide education about family planning.

Economic Dualism – This occurs when a country has a technologically advanced and technologically retarded sectors existing together.

Technologically advanced	Technologically retarded
Finance	Cottage industry
Insurance	Small businesses
Petroleum	Manufacturing
Mining	Peasant farming

Foreign investment

Foreign Direct Investment (FDI) – This is the investment into a business by a person or company in another country.

Foreign Indirect Investment – This is the investment into a business by a person or company in another country through buying shares on the stock exchange.

Benefits of foreign investment

1. It creates a greater production of goods or services in the country.
2. It creates employment for persons living in the country.
3. Higher-income leads to economic growth and a better quality of life for citizens.
4. The country benefits from greater international trade and national income

Disadvantages of foreign investment

1. The profits of foreign companies are sent back home when made.
2. The foreign company can decide to leave at any time which can lead to loss of jobs.
3. Foreign companies can push local companies out of business and create monopolies in the market.

Business Technology

This refers to the application of a wide range of software, hardware, and services that keep a business running to ensure efficiency and smooth operation of all business activities. The main goal of technology is to bring about change that positively affects the business and society.

The role of Information Communication Technology (ICT) in business

ICT is the use of digital technology to store, process, analyze, and manipulate data. It simply helps individuals, businesses, and organizations to use reliable information.

Ways technology influences banking and commerce

i. **Automatic Teller Machines (ATMs) and Automated Banking Machines (ABMs)** – These machines make it convenient for customers to deposits and withdraw money without going to the bank.

ii. **Online banking** – This enables customers to access their accounts from home and other locations using personal computers. This facility enables customers to access their account activities from the comfort of their homes and permits easy and convenient payment of utility and other bills.

iii. **Electronic commerce (e-commerce)** – This enables business transactions to be made via the World-wide-web, using the internet, without visiting any store. Customers can search for products online, buy and get them delivered.

Types of technology
- a. **Traditional technology**
- i. **Productivity tools**, for example, Word, Excel, Access, PowerPoint, and Photoshop.
- ii. **Specialist applications:**
  - **Accounting:** QuickBooks – This is a software designed to manage payroll, inventory, sales, and other needs of a small business.
  - **Computer-Aided Design** (CAD) – This is the use of computer technology to aid in the creation, documentation, and modification of designs. It is used by architects, engineers, drafters, artists, and others to create drawings.
  - **Management Information Systems** – This is a computer system that makes management decisions with the data and information collected from different areas of a business.
- b. **Digital communication technologies:**
  - i. **Internet** – A global computer network that connects computer systems across the globe. It provides a variety of information and communication.
  - ii. **Mobile** – A device that is used to facilitate communication, for example, the cell phone.

E-commerce and e-business

Always keep in mind that the 'E' means Electronic which involves internet and electronic data.

1. **E-commerce** is the buying and selling of goods and services

using the internet.
2. **E-business** includes the buying and selling of goods and services online, with the support of customer service. It reduces costs by not having an actual front office business.

Ways in which technology can improve business efficiency:
a) **Speed and time** – The use of technology increases the speed at which manual tasks would have been completed and therefore saves time in the business operation.
b) **Easier storage** – Technology eliminates the need for physical storage as documents and files can be stored softcopy using cloud technology which reduces the space needed for storage.
c) **Improved sharing of information** – Using technology such as the intranet, employees can share important documents without having to transfer physical documents.
d) **Automation** - Technology allows tasks to be completed with minimal human assistance by allowing some tasks to be computerized.

Benefits of technology to business
a) It allows buyers to reach more potential customers by advertising and developing a business relationship via social marketing techniques such as Facebook, YouTube, etc.
b) It connects various operations of the business, which helps to reduce the business costs and improve efficiency and profitability.
c) It provides better service to customers by being accessible at any time with 24/7 online customer support or by digitalizing

the purchasing experience for customers. For example, PDR. Institute or Amazon.

d) It supports better relationships with key partners in a timely manner as information needed can be accessed at any time using different technology platforms.

Consequences of unethical use of ICT

a) **Security** – Hackers can easily hack into a computer system when it's connected to the internet.

b) **Privacy** – While technology allows us to find and share information, a person's privacy can be exploited by the use of internet webcams and social media networks.

c) **Intellectual property infringement** – Information technology has allowed easy access to some products like music, artworks, and books to be used without payment.

d) **Impact on humans** – Since IT systems must run all the time, it can lead to stress and work overload on IT experts which can lead to errors being made.

Factors that determine a country's standard of living and its quality of life

a. **Indicators of a country's standard of living (SOL):**

i. The level of consumption of goods and services.

ii. An average disposable income of the population – Disposable income is the remaining money after the reduction of taxes and pension payments. One can either spend or save this at wish.

iii. The level of national ownership of property and other assets such as businesses, homes, trucks, and other equipment.

- iv. Access to modern-day technology such as high-speed internet and other devices.
- v. The level of investment in research and technology for the improvement of business operations.
   - b. **Indicators of quality of life (QOL)**
- i. The extent of **security enjoyed** based on the level of crime.
- ii. The availability of **health care**, educational and recreational facilities.
- iii. The push for **healthy diet** and nutrition.
   - c. **Life expectancy** – This is the average amount of years an individual is expected to live.
- i. The rate of **infant mortality** – The number of children under the age of one (1) that die every year.
     - ii. Access to **public utilities**, such as electricity, clean water, good roads, and enhanced technology.

This POB Handbook has been created in line with the recently revised 2019 CSEC syllabus and incorporates the new trends within the field of business.

Key features include:
- Full coverage of the CSEC syllabus that ensures students are ready for the examination. Easy to read and understand all topics covered in the syllabus.
- Provides global examples to enhance students' understanding of topics covered in the handbook. Caribbean examples are provided with relevant information covered.

Ajillah Sinnette-Vincent has been an educator for the last 12 years, having taught at both the University and Secondary school level in Trinidad and Tobago. She continues to pursue her passion for excellence in teaching and learning daily as her life goal.

CSEC is a registered trademark of the Caribbean Examination Council (CXC). Principles of Business Road to Success POB Handbook is an independent publication and has not been approved or otherwise sponsored by CXC.

PDR Institute

www.ingramcontent.com/pod-product-compliance
Lightning Source LLC
Chambersburg PA
CBHW050009230526
45465CB00003BB/1339